MIGHTY MEN
STAY ON TRACK

RICK SCARBOROUGH
FOREWORD BY LT. GENERAL GERALD BOYKIN

MIGHTY MEN
STAY ON TRACK

RICK SCARBOROUGH

21stCENTURY
P R E S S
READING YOU LOUD AND CLEAR

SPRINGFIELD, MISSOURI

MIGHTY MEN STAY ON TRACK

Published by 21st Century Press
Springfield, MO 65807

21st Century Press and Heritage Builders Publishing are Christian publishers dedicated to publishing books that have a high standard of family values. We believe the vision for our partnership is to provide families and individuals with user-friendly materials that will help them in their daily lives and experiences. It is our prayer that this book will help you discover Biblical truth for your own life and help you meet the needs of others. May God richly bless you.

21st Century Press
2131 W. Republic Rd.
PMB 211
Springfield, MO 65807

Cover and Book Design: Lee Fredrickson

ISBN: 978-0-9981392-0-3 Softcover Edition
       978-0-9863864-9-7 Hardback Edition

Visit our website at: www.heritagebuilderspublishing.com
Printed in the United States of America

DEDICATION

This book is dedicated to my sweet daughter, Kathryn Anne, who finished her assignment on Earth October 27, 2004, at the tender age of 25. She cared for hurting people more than any individual I have ever been privileged to know. The reason she cared so much for them is that she was called upon by her Lord to suffer much during her brief time on earth.

At the age of 18, she was diagnosed with an acute bipolar disorder. She battled the disease until her death seven years later. Her last four years of life were her best years, and she left many friends who were deeply impacted by her servant spirit.

I chose to use track events to convey spiritual lessons in this book, because Kathryn was a track star, excelling in long distance. In fact, she was a world-class runner who was just entering her prime when the Father called her home. She showed promise as a long distance runner during her freshman year of high school, when she placed 5th in district competition running against seniors. But running took too much time and her basketball coach demanded that she give up running if she was going to play for him on the varsity girls basketball team. Her talents in basketball were never sufficient to overcome her 5 foot 5-inch frame, so she sat the bench most of her high school career. No one who ever saw her on the court doubted her dedication to the sport and she was an excellent defender, but her shooting, unfortunately, never measured up.

When we discovered she was bipolar during the days just before she was to enter college, we were all devastated, knowing little about mental illness at the time. As we began processing her illness and trying to understand it, she fell into deep depression. One evening she and I went for a ride and ended up on Galveston Island. When I asked her, "Kat, what would you truly like to do with your life?" Her reply caught me by surprise; "I wish I had never given up cross country, Dad. I could have been very good at that."

That evening I called her high school track coach and told him what she said, and he agreed. He then took the time to arrange for us to meet Coach Al Lawrence, the legendary long-distance runner, and former Olympian, who set several world records during his running career before becoming the head track coach for the University of Houston Cougars. After retiring, he began training runners at Memorial Park in Houston. He took a special interest in Kathryn, and soon she was running every day at Memorial Park, under his supervision.

There isn't space to list all of her accomplishments over the following years, nor all of her setbacks due to the illness, especially during the first three years. The medications required to balance and stabilize bipolar people are harsh and dangerous. The most effective drugs in this ever-developing field of study are sodium based, meaning that the patient typically gains weight with the medication. Weight gain is hard for any young woman but particularly difficult for someone competing in long distance running. Kathryn was a determined runner and during the ensuing years, she ran for the University of Houston, helping the cross country team win the Conference Championship. Later, she ran for the Stephen F. Austin Lumberjack Cross Country Team which also won a conference championship.

At the conclusion of both University team competitions, Kathryn would end up in the hospital due to the tremendous pressure and exertion required to run competitively. Her mom and I would hold her and cry with her during those times. Seeing her struggle and hurt was simply overwhelming.

Then our dear friend, Freddie Gage, an evangelist who took a special interest in Kathryn, introduced us to Paul Meier, a renowned psychiatrist, who worked with premier athletes who suffered from mental illness. He recommended that Kathryn be placed on some experimental medications that were not sodium based. That began four wonderful years during which Kathryn ran her first and second Houston Marathons, an annual event that draws runners from around the nation and over 26,000 runners in all.

In her first attempt, Kathryn was the ninth woman to finish the grueling race. In her second attempt, she was the second female overall, trailing a professional runner from out of state, and the first amateur female to finish, earning the right to represent Houston in Greece later that year. She passed on that honor due to attending college classes.

She also began competing in the 50K distance, a race of over 35 miles. She reached national ranking status and was featured on the cover of Texas Runners Magazine for her accomplishments. All under the guidance of Coach Al, who has become a special member of our family.

She was never completely free from occasional setbacks, but by 2004, we believed that she was on her way to a wonderful life of dealing with a difficult but manageable disease. Then in October, we grew increasingly concerned for her. On the night of October 26, we prayed with her before retiring for we knew she was struggling. I checked on her several times through the night. She lived in a wing of our house during that time. At seven I got up for the day and she was fine. Then at 7:15 AM my wife began screaming, and I rushed into Kathryn's room, where I found her mother holding her lifeless body. I applied CPR as best I could, but to no avail. Medics arrived shortly and pronounced her dead. I will never forget that day as long as I live.

Because she died in our home, an autopsy was required by law. They discovered no overdose of medication nor any unnatural cause of death. They speculated that due to her regimen of medications for her illness, coupled with running up to 70 miles a week to stay competitive in ultra long distance competition, that her heart just gave out.

And what a heart she had. Kathryn was always bringing hurting people to our home for ministry. She made us live out what she had heard us teach and preach throughout her life. This love for the hurting opened our doors to several people, whose lives were in shambles, that she met through running or on the street, only to see them move out months later in pursuit of the Savior that Kathryn told them about. Several of them were present for her funeral as were many from the Houston runners world. I got to baptize two of her special projects in our church.

She left us with stacks of journals filled with both her struggles and her victories. She lived in constant praise and adoration of her Savior, sprinkled with trips into deep and dark depression, resulting in several stays in hospitals, where she would regain her balance. But when she died, we were caught by surprise, because we earnestly thought we were beyond those dark days.

She's been gone for over eleven years, and I still cry when I let myself think too much about her. I miss her, but I know where she is, and I know I will see her again. She won a room full of trophies that we keep in storage, but the trophy she got when she saw Jesus on October 27, 2004, is the one we treasure the most. Kathryn was a treasure. Kathryn was a champion. Kathryn was looking for a Mighty Man to marry when she got promoted to see the Mightiest Man of all...Jesus.

On the morning of her death, next to her bed, she wrote down the following verse on a three by five card: "I have fought the good fight, I have finished the race, I have kept the faith" (2 Timothy 4:7).

This book is dedicated to her. Dad.

CONTENTS

FOREWORD

By Lt. General Gerald Boykin

Upon retiring from the U.S. Army in 2007, I left the Pentagon and moved to a small town in south central Virginia to teach at one of the two remaining all-male colleges in America, Hampden-Sydney College. The school was founded in 1775, making it the tenth oldest college or university in the nation. It has remained all male in spite of continuous efforts by feminist and liberal groups to force it to accept coeds. Currently, there are over forty all-female colleges across the country, yet there appears to be little pressure for them to accept men. Why are male colleges now down to only two in the nation? The answer in part is that the nation has been experiencing an all out assault on masculinity for decades now.

Society constantly bombards men with a message that they are no different from women and that their role in society can and should be the same as that of women. Men are confused and demoralized, and American society is suffering as a result. Look at the fatherless homes throughout the nation where children grow up with no positive male role models or worse yet, destructive and abusive role models. This problem of absentee fathers is epidemic now as many men see themselves as simply sperm donors with no responsibility for investing in their children's lives. According to data from the U.S. Census Bureau, of the 24 million children in America, one out of three, live in homes where the biological father is absent. This course cannot continue if this nation expects to survive. America needs real men, men of character, Godly Mighty Men.

My father was a Mighty Man who knew what a man was supposed to be and acted like a Mighty Man throughout his life. Wounded on D-Day, Gerald Boykin was blind in his left eye for life. You would never have known it though since he refused to let his injuries slow him down or hold him back. He was a role model for his three children, always spending time with them, coaching their athletic teams, and sharing his wisdom and experiences to help them develop into good citizens who loved America and committed themselves to service to the Lord. He never graduated from high school, but he was self-taught and well read. Gerald never wanted anything but opportunity; not a hand out or charity, just opportunity. Among his values were hard work and making one's own way in life without complaint. He was a Mighty Man and a tremendous mentor. How many of our youth today have a Mighty Man for their mentor? Too few, is the obvious answer, which is why America is experiencing such turmoil in the family structure as families are disintegrating and society is suffering. Mighty Men are hard to find.

Most historians believe that the modern Olympic games are derived from the Olympic games that occurred every four years in ancient Greece, beginning in 776 BC. Greek legend also holds that these ancient sporting events took place in the sanctuary of Zeus in Olympia, Greece. Competitors were athletes from the myriad city-states and kingdoms of ancient Greece, and these contests continued until the 5th century AD. The competition included foot races, a pentathlon (discus, javelin, boxing, racing, wrestling, and jumping), equestrian events, pankration, and multiple running events. These games were religious events as well as athletic competition between the top athletes of a culture that valued manhood and the warrior ethos. Participants were Mighty Men.

In a sense, these games were a form of warfare among ancient warriors, as many of these competitors were enemies who had previously met or could, in the future, meet in battle as the various societies within Greece struggled for supremacy. In fact, it was standard practice for all warfare among city-states and kingdoms to be suspended for the duration of the games and travelers to the Olympics were given safe passage to attend or participate in the games. The Greeks valued Mighty Men who they saw as the hope of their people in both warfare and athletics. The Greeks depended on Mighty Men to preserve and defend their culture and way of life. Athletics was simply a symbol of the warrior ethos that was expected of men in ancient Greece. Can America lay claim to a culture of Mighty Men today? In my view, our country is not even sure what a man is anymore.

Like the early Olympics, the concept of the marathon was a creation of ancient Greece. Legend holds that this 26.2-mile run represents the distance that the Greek warrior Phillippides ran after the battle of Marathon to notify the people of Athens that the Persians had been defeated by the Greek army. Phillippides most likely had participated in the battle of Marathon against probably the greatest army in the world at the time, the army of the Persian Empire. In 1896, the marathon became part of the modern Olympics although the distance was not standardized until 1921 when Olympic organizers settled on 26.2 miles. Every four years now people of all nations pause to watch and cheer for their nation's athletes as both the Summer and Winter Olympics capture world attention.

Like everyone, I enjoy watching the world's finest young men and women athletes compete in venues around the globe where wins are often determined by fractions of a second, where athletes who have trained for most of their lives for this moment put everything they have on the line in hopes of a victory. I have often pondered whether these Olympians are born with natural athletic skills or whether they have just spent their lives developing their bodies and honing their skills. Obviously, it is both. Competing in the Olympics demands a tremendous personal discipline and total commitment to a cause.

Similarly, Christian men need to be disciplined and committed to developing spiritually into serious followers of Christ. Think about it for a moment. There is so much to learn from the world of athletics, especially Track and Field which was the foundation of both ancient and modern Olympics. Individual preparation for competition in the Christian life is no different than preparing for a race. A Christian man must have a concept for how he will prepare for spiritual warfare and a life of service to Christ. Moreover, he then must be determined and disciplined enough to stay with his plan and to overcome setbacks and hardships along the way.

So many men in America have lost their ability to deal with hardship and difficulty, especially in the Christian life. This nation was built by Mighty Men who were not deterred by hardship, who were not afraid of the unknown, and who stayed focused on their ultimate objective; a new nation.

As a college football player, I wrongly assumed that my sons would love the game as I did and would follow my lead and play the game that gave me an education. But neither of my two boys showed much interest in the gridiron and neither became a star quarterback or defensive guard as I was. However, my youngest son, Aaron, did become a high school track star. He was fast on his feet and had a lot of natural ability, but he was also dedicated to the sport. He trained hard and showed a tremendous commitment to being the best athlete on the field. No one could beat him out of the starting blocks, and he always finished a step ahead of his competition. In the relays, he was the anchor. If his team was behind, he made up the difference to bring home the gold. I learned a great deal watching him and realized that he was developing a lifestyle that would ensure success in his future endeavors. And indeed I was correct. After five years in the U.S. Army after college, Aaron became a Secret Service agent who has excelled in the performance of his job of protecting the most powerful man in the world, the U.S. President. More importantly, he is a committed Christian who runs the race of life just as he did the 440-yard dash or the relay in high school. His early lessons from Track and Field have helped mold him into a Mighty Man.

This book, *Mighty Men Stay on Track*, is the most unique book I have seen for men. Dr. Scarborough uses Track and Field as a metaphor for nearly every situation in life and society to show men what God requires of us. It should be instructive that the great Apostle Paul used the same metaphor in his final days to refer to his life when he said in 2 Timothy 4:7 "I am already being poured out like a drink offering, and the time of my departure is at hand, I have fought the good fight, I have finished the race, I have kept the faith." Paul recognized that his time was short and that he would soon leave this world to be united with his Lord. Yet Paul compared his life's work to warfare and athletics. Clearly, he fought the good fight and finished the race well. Did Paul know about the Olympic games in Greece? Most likely he did, given that Greek was such an important language in his time; even to the point that the Gospels were written in Greek. He was a Mighty Man, wise and well informed of the events and issues of his time. Everyone for centuries to come would be able to relate to his comparison of his life to a race and would understand his reference to "finishing the race."

In *Mighty Men Stay on Track*, Dr. Scarborough coaches the reader on how to live as a Christian man, who wants to be able to say the same thing that Paul did, when he nears the end. Filled with pertinent scriptures, Mighty Men deals with all aspects of the Christian life. The book explains how a man is supposed to treat his wife and family and how to deal with conflict. Dr. Scarborough discusses the differences between men and women and how they communicate or better stated, why men don't communicate. This book takes the reader through the imperative for managing personal time and using that time wisely and in a balanced fashion. Essentially, this is a book that touches every aspect of life that men ask questions about or that they struggle with.

In my thirty-six years in the US Army, I saw combat on four continents. Because I was in Special Operations most of that time, I served with the very best that the U.S. Military had to offer. Men of uncommon valor were common among the Delta Force and Special Forces units in which I was privileged to serve. They were Mighty Men who knew the cause they were serving and were willing to die for it. And some of them did die for the transcendent cause that made them such Mighty Men. In almost every case, they died for their teammates or their fellow warriors in places like Iran, Panama, Grenada, Mogadishu, or Iraq.

These men never died because they were unprepared for war. They trained hard and took their preparations seriously. Christian men must do the same in preparing for the struggles and challenges of life. Every Christian man must know what he believes and what price he is willing to pay for his beliefs.

An ever-increasing atheist/Marxist movement in America is challenging all Christian beliefs today. America needs now more than ever these Mighty Men who can lead in the families, the communities, and in the public square. Such men with a biblical worldview can change the direction of the nation and restore the founding principles that were handed down by the Mighty Men who created America.

PREFACE

King David is, without a doubt, one of the greatest men who ever lived, and as a leader knows few peers. Beginning with his confronting the giant Goliath, David's life of courage and valor inspired men to live and die for him. During his lifetime he subdued his enemies and ushered in an era of peace and prosperity in Israel, unparalleled in all of her incredible history.

This book is about Mighty Men, and how America needs another generation of Mighty Men, who, like David and his band of thirty-seven heroes, inspired an entire nation to greatness. Men today do not know who they are. They have been feminized and sent to the back of the bus. Our universities are disproportionately filled with women, while men, too tepid to push back, are dropping out. Instead of an education, they are opting for video games and singleness in a nation where many women have cheapened their uniqueness as they have pushed men aside. Before we go on, let me introduce you to...

Thirty-seven Mighty Men.

In the *Message Bible* we find the listing of David's Mighty Men.

Josheb-Basshebeth, the Tahkemonite. He was chief of the Three. He once put his spear to work against eight hundred—killed them all in a day.

Eleazar son of Dodai the Ahohite was the next of the elite Three. He was with David when the Philistines poked fun at them at Pas Dammim. When the Philistines drew up for battle, Israel retreated. But Eleazar stood his ground and killed Philistines right and left until he was exhausted—but he never let go of his sword! A big win for God that day. The army then rejoined Eleazar, but all there was left to do was the cleanup.

Shammah son of Agee the Hararite was the third of the Three. The Philistines had mustered for battle at Lehi, where there was a field full of lentils. Israel fled before the Philistines, but Shammah took his stand at the center of the field, successfully defended it, and routed the Philistines. Another great victory for God!

One day during harvest, the Three parted from the Thirty and joined David at the Cave of Adullam. A squad of Philistines had set up camp in the Valley of Rephaim. While David was holed up in the Cave, the Philistines had their base camp in Bethlehem. David had a sudden craving and said, "Would I ever like a drink of water from the well at the gate of Bethlehem!" So the Three penetrated the Philistine lines, drew water from the well at the gate of Bethlehem, and brought it back to David. But David wouldn't drink it; he poured it out as an offering to God, saying, "There is no way, God, that I'll drink this! This isn't mere water, it's their life-blood—they risked their very lives to bring it!" So David refused to drink it.

This is the sort of thing that the Three did.

Abishai brother of Joab and son of Zeruiah was the head of the Thirty. He once got credit for killing three hundred with his spear, but he was never named in the same breath as the Three. He was the most respected of the Thirty and was their captain, but never got included among the Three.

Benaiah son of Jehoiada from Kabzeel was a vigorous man who accomplished a great deal. He once killed two lion cubs in Moab. Another time, on a snowy day, he climbed down into a pit and killed a lion. Another time, he killed a formidable Egyptian. The Egyptian was armed with a spear and Benaiah went against him with nothing but a walking stick; he seized the spear from his grip and killed him with his own spear.

These are the things that Benaiah son of Jehoiada is famous for. But neither did he ever get ranked with the Three. He was held in greatest respect among the Thirty, but he never got included with the Three. David put him in charge of his bodyguard.

The Thirty

"The Thirty" consisted of: Asahel brother of Joab Elhanan son of Dodo of Bethlehem; Shammah the Harodite; Elika the Harodite; Helez the Paltite; Ira son of Ikkesh the Tekoite; Abiezer the Anathothite; Sibbecai the Hushathite; Zalmon the Ahohite; Maharai the Netophathite; Heled son of Baanah the Netophathite; Ithai son of Ribai from Gibeah of the Benjaminites; Benaiah the Pirathonite; Hiddai from the badlands of Gaash; Abi-Albon the Arbathite; Azmaveth the Barhumite; Eliahba the Shaalbonite; Jashen the Gizonite; Jonathan son of Shammah the Hararite; Ahiam son of Sharar the Urite; Eliphelet son of Ahasbai the Maacathite; Eliam son of Ahithophel the Gilonite; Hezro the Carmelite; Paarai the Arbite; Igal son of Nathan, commander of the army of Hagrites; Zelek the Ammonite; Naharai the Beerothite, weapon bearer of Joab son of Zeruiah; Ira the Ithrite; Gareb the Ithrite; Uriah the Hittite. Thirty-seven, all told (2 Samuel 23:8-39).

Mighty Men, one and all.

These were men of exploits who inspired a nation. We must find men like that in America today. In 1992, I got involved in taking my faith beyond the boundaries of the local church I was pastoring. During that year I discovered a group of like minded men who were faithfully resisting America's slide toward Gomorrah. One of those mighty men was the late Dr. Jerry Falwell, who discovered that I was standing up against the ungodly actions of our local school board and administration, as well as our city council. He started requesting that I come to his major pastor events around the country and share my testimony of how, as a local pastor, I had mobilized our church family to begin voting their values in local elections and urging leaders to run for public office. By 1996, members of our church occupied the majority of seats on our local school board and city council, and both the police chief and the city manager had joined our church. They did this purely because they saw a local church get involved in civil affairs, striving to make its community a better place for people to rear their children.

In 1998, I formed a ministry to encourage other pastors to do as I had done while pastoring First Baptist Church, Pearland, and begin mobilizing their congregations. I asked Dr. Falwell to assist me, and he suggested building an Advisory Board of national religious leaders, who would lend their wisdom and provide me with credibility with other pastors. Dr. Falwell personally enlisted Dr. D. James Kennedy, Dr. Tim LaHaye, Viet Nam War Hero and double amputee, Evangelist Tim Lee, Rev. Don Wildmon, Dr. Adrian Rogers, among others, who consented to serve as my advisors. All of them were Mighty Men, from whom I learned so much about what it means to stand up against all odds for that which you believe.

Over the past two decades since, I have met many Mighty Men in America. I am reticent to use names for fear of offending some I don't mention, but there are many. One whom I will name is Dr. James Dobson. I know of no man alive today nor who has lived during my lifetime, who has displayed more courage nor taken more heat for his beliefs, yet without ever wavering, than Jim. He truly is a Mighty Man.

Another Mighty Man, whom I have come to admire and deeply appreciate, is Lt. Gen. (Ret.) William G. "Jerry" Boykin who now serves as Family Research Council's Executive Vice President.

He was one of the original members of the U.S. Army's Delta Force. He was privileged to ultimately command these elite warriors in combat operations. Later, Jerry Boykin commanded all the Army's Green Berets as well as the Special Warfare Center and School.

In all, Lt. Gen. Boykin spent 36 years in the Army, serving his last four years as the Deputy Undersecretary of Defense for Intelligence. During his 36-year career in the military, he spent 13 years in the Delta Force, including two years as its commander. He was involved in numerous high-profile missions, including the 1980 Iran hostage rescue attempt, the 1992 hunt for Pablo Escobar in Colombia, and the Black Hawk Down incident in Mogadishu, Somalia.

He is an author and teaches at Hampden-Sydney College, Virginia. He is an ordained minister with a passion for spreading the Gospel of Jesus Christ and encouraging Christians to become warriors in God's Kingdom.

I cannot overstate the sense of good fortune and blessing I have had as a result of standing in the shadows of such men during my lifetime. It is often said, you become like the people you spend the most time with. Look at your friends and make a list of men you most admire and ask yourself, "Do they qualify to be called Mighty Men?" If not, perhaps you may want to find a few new friends. I have spent a lifetime trying to read biographies of great men of the past and have benefited immensely from doing so.

That's what this book is about. Becoming a Mighty Man who stays on track. I have used track metaphors to teach spiritual lessons, but in the final analysis, this book is designed to find the secret of becoming a Mighty Man. May you be encouraged to become one as you work your way through the following chapters. You are God's plan for saving America.

Chapter ONE

HOW TO ACHIEVE SUCCESS IN LIFE

"The Long Jump"

I have had a personal fascination and love for politics that began in high school and continues to the present day. I know that sounds crazy, but I have always enjoyed following political races and politicians, and even planned a career in politics myself at one time. I was well into earning a double major in political science and speech, good preparation for law school, which is where I was headed before God informed me He had better plans for my life. I especially enjoyed following men like Governor Mike Huckabee, whom I have much respect for and whom I believe would make our country a great President, if given the chance. I first met Gov. Huckabee while he and I were attending Southwestern Baptist Theological Seminary in Ft. Worth, Texas and was delighted and surprised, when I heard he had run for Lt. Governor in Arkansas and won. I had long advocated for Pastors supporting men and women of character running for public office as a major component in restoring our nation, and was thrilled when I heard that Mike was the new Lt. Governor of Arkansas.

But over the years I have had a growing awareness that no politician nor political party is going to save America. That's why I wrote this book. You, sir, are America's best hope for national renewal, both politically and spiritually. Our founders knew the secret to America's greatness was found in her citizens. Men, committed to Christ, are the best hope we have for restoring our country and returning it to the values that our Founders knew were essential for America to fulfill her destiny. Our great nation was established on the principles of liberty and self-government and the belief, that God, not the government, granted men the right to life, liberty and the pursuit of happiness.

Throughout this book, I will be using track and field events as a teaching tool to convey spiritual truths and encourage you to develop spiritual disciplines in your life that will empower you to become one of God's "Mighty" Men. The athletes mentioned to convey life lessons are not all Christians, but they are among the greatest in their respective competitions. We can't all be champions in the field of athletics, but we can be something far more satisfying—Champions for Christ.

As we examine the long jump, we see principles that can help us be successful in life. Carl Lewis, the greatest long jump champion in history, made choices in life that disappointed many of his fans, but the lessons he taught us in the long jump are still worth considering.

God desires that every man succeeds in life. Scripture reveals His plan for you and me: "For I know the plans I have for you," declares the Lord, "plans to prosper you and not to harm you, plans to give you hope and a future" (Jeremiah 29:11). But not every man succeeds in life because many refuse to allow God to mold and shape their lives. God does not compare us to each other, but rather every man is held to the standard of God's Word and is accountable for how he uses the skills and potential that God has given him. God is watching to see whether we use our gifts and abilities to advance His purposes or for self-advancement and personal gratification.

Hebrews 12:1-2 says, "Therefore since we are surrounded by such a great cloud of witnesses, let us throw off everything that hinders, and the sin that so easily entangles, and let us run with perseverance the race marked out for us. Let us fix our eyes on Jesus, the author and finisher of our faith, who for the joy set before Him endured the cross, scorning its shame and sat down at the right hand of the throne of God."

In the New Testament, the Apostle Paul often used athletic contests to illustrate spiritual truths. Being a former college athlete myself, I can relate to those passages, but you don't have to be an athlete to benefit from Paul's wisdom. The authorship of Hebrews is uncertain, but one thing we do know is that the Holy Spirit was ultimately responsible.

Achieving the 'Impossible'

The legendary Carl Lewis, who is among the greatest Olympians, qualified for five consecutive U.S. Olympic teams, beginning in 1980, and competed in four successive Olympics—1984, 1988, 1992 and 1996 (the U.S. boycotted the 1980 Olympics under President Jimmy Carter). He won gold medals each time, accumulating a total of 10 medals including nine golds. He was crowned the Olympic long jump champion for twelve consecutive years and achieved what most thought was impossible.

At the age of 35, when he won his fourth gold medal in the long jump, few of the "experts" thought he should even be competing. They often reminded him that he was too old to expect to compete against younger athletes. It was not until his final attempt in the prelims that he jumped far enough to qualify for the finals at the 1996 Olympics.

Carl Lewis and the long jump event illustrate, "How to Achieve Success in Life." So, how can we achieve such success in our lives? In essence, that's what this entire book is about.

My ministry began as the part-time youth pastor at First Baptist Church in historic Nacogdoches, Texas, while I was attending Stephen F. Austin University on a football scholarship from 1968-1971. Nacogdoches is the oldest town in Texas, nestled deep in the piney woods of East Texas. I met my wife, Tommye Glyn Adams, a life-long resident of Nacogdoches, while attending SFA, and we were married on December 27, 1970.

I have been very fortunate in that I have experienced few days in which I dreaded getting out of bed to go to work. I watched my father throughout his entire working life go to a job that he disliked. But he never failed to arrive on time and often early, because he accepted it as his duty so he could provide for his family. I respect and admire him for that. But I am saddened when I consider how much better his life could have been, had he found a job early on that was his passion in life.

I remember the first time I was paid for speaking in a church. I was promoted as a college football player who loved Jesus. After the service, the pastor handed me an envelope, and I opened it thinking that it was a thank you note. To my surprise, that envelope held a $25 check. I walked outside, overwhelmed to the point of tears that someone would pay me for doing something I would gladly have done for free. I loved the Lord and wanted to share what He had done for me with anyone who would listen. I never considered being paid for it.

I have been blessed to live my entire adult life doing what I love: preaching and sharing the Gospel. While I am not a wealthy man by the world's standard, I don't know of a single thing the world offers that I feel I've missed out on by preaching. I have experienced a joyful life with my wife Tommye, my beloved soul mate and best friend, doing what we love to do. That's what I consider a successful life.

I realize that many men reading this book will identify more with my father than with me. Many men haven't reached a point that they know what they want to do with their life while still in the preparation phase, and consequently, miss the opportunity to prepare for a profession about which they are passionate. If you're in that category, you're the man I wrote this book to encourage. You can be happy and fruitful IF you adopt a simple strategy. Starting now, live every day in communion and partnership with God. Scripture says, "And whatever you do, whether in word or deed, do it all in the name of the Lord Jesus, giving thanks to God the Father through Him" (Colossians 3:17). Paul also wrote: "So whether you eat or drink or whatever you do, do it all for the glory of God" (1 Corinthians 10:31).

A New Approach

Recognize that God does not make mistakes. We make them all the time, but He never does. I discovered a principle in the Apostle Paul's letter to the Philippians. This discovery gave me a new perspective on life while playing football at Stephen F. Austin University in the late 1960s. It reads, "For it is God who is at work in you, both to will and to work for His good pleasure. Do all things without grumbling or disputing; so that you will prove yourselves to be blameless and innocent, children of God above reproach in the midst of a crooked and perverse generation, among whom you appear as lights in the world" (Philippians 2:13-15 NAB).

I fell under deep conviction by the Holy Spirit that even though I was a Christian who regularly attended church, I was no different from the rest of the team when we were on the football practice field during late August, with the sun baking us in 100-degree heat amplified by 90% humidity. Like everybody else, I dreaded workouts and grumbled about the heat and intensity of the workouts.

After reading that it was God who was working His will and good pleasure in everything that I did, I decided to try a new approach. I gave my workouts to Jesus and decided to view each day as an opportunity to serve the Lord. Instead of remaining in the ranks of the "whiners" who complained about how hot it was and the length of our two-a-day workouts, I began to look for ways to share my faith.

If you feel trapped in a job that brings you neither joy nor satisfaction, give it to Jesus. Determine in your mind and heart that it's His job until He gives you a better one. God specializes in miracles, and He can make your workplace, assuming it doesn't compromise your Christian values, a vehicle of ministry to advance His purposes on the earth. You can learn the joy of being paid for doing something you love as certainly as I have, IF you view your job as your ministry. Then, every day, you can get up knowing that God is going to use you to advance His kingdom.

IF you will give God the job you're currently in, and view every co-worker as your personal mission field, you'll see your job from Heaven's perspective. Your co-workers are not robots; they are precious individuals for whom Jesus died. Once you realize that, everything changes. Now you're looking at your job from the vantage point of a "Mighty Man."

The Apostle Paul exhorted the believers in Philippi to: "Do all things without grumbling or disputing," and promised them that if they did, they would "appear as lights in the world." One translator puts it this way: "you will shine like the stars in the sky."

With God's help, I began cracking jokes about the heat and encouraging my teammates to focus on the greater goal, which was to win football games and make our university proud. As a result of this new attitude, everything changed. Soon, my teammates realized that my faith was real and that I was different—different in a way that made their world better and easier to endure. I wasn't some oddball Christian; I was a teammate seeking to lighten the load and make the team better.

It wasn't long until the whole atmosphere changed in our workouts and locker room. And it paid off on the field. Our offense became one of the most explosive offenses in the history of Stephen F. Austin, setting records that stood many years. Four players received an opportunity to play professional football, which is unheard of for a small college like SFA. But I think I received the highest honor of all. I got to stand before thousands of students across the nation for many years, using the platform of college football to tell them about Jesus.

If we do our part, God will do His part. He is always faithful.

Far too often, Christians are different in all the wrong ways. Jesus was beloved by sinners and scorned by the religious types in His day. We should seek to be winsome, especially in the workplace. Many of those we rub shoulders with for hours each day have walked away from the church because they met too many pseudo-Christians who exuded anything but happiness and joy. Many co-workers will never have a chance to see a real Christian if you fail to live an authentic Christian life before them, and you can't do that if you're complaining just like them. Ask God to show you the big picture, about your workplace. After all, it is your ministry we are talking about. That's what Mighty Men do!

My wife and I were encouraged by one of our Pastors to select a verse of Scripture before we got married, upon which we would base our marriage. We selected Matthew 6:33 as our "life verse": "But seek first His kingdom and His righteousness, and all these things will be given to you as well." Many years later, I can testify that Matthew 6:33 works. Try it where you work, live and play.

I believe that God intends every man's life to be full and meaningful. In fact, it was Jesus who said, "I have come that you may have life, and have it to the fullest" (John 10:10). Does that mean it's supposed to be all fun and games? No, not at all. Does it mean that you will always be happy? No. But I do believe a life lived in consecration to Jesus will inherently produce an abundance of joy and contentment. I know that to be true because I've seen it in my life and the life of others. In an ideal situation, a person will discover what God wants them to be early in life. But if not, our God is the God of the second chance, and more if needed and genuinely sought.

Equipping Yourself

Mighty Men have to make choices in life. Carl Lewis could have decided to throw the shot put instead of competing in the long jump. With his commitment and work ethic, he likely would have done better than most, but he would never have won four gold medals over sixteen years of competition in the shot put. God did not physically equip him to achieve the same greatness in the shot put as he did in the long jump. He had to discover what he could do best and prepare for it.

So, how do we determine what we're best equipped to do?

First, we should listen to our own heart.

Why trudge through life doing something you hate doing? Life is too short to be miserable. One reason there are so many long faces in this world is that so many men are just trying to survive. Henry David Thoreau, whom I would not cite as a role model, nonetheless put it memorably in 1854 in his famous book Walden: "The mass of men lead lives of quiet desperation. What is called resignation is confirmed desperation."

Why live that way? Your heart will tell you a lot about what God has equipped you to do in life by the passion you find there. I am not proposing that one's heart is the final word, for the Bible says that the heart is desperately wicked before being surrendered to Christ (Jer. 17:9). But we also know that God's Word says: "Whether you turn to the right or the left, you will hear a voice behind you saying, 'This is the way, walk in it'" (Isaiah 30:21). We should listen to our hearts.

Secondly, we should listen to others.

I would say that it's safe to assume that someone encouraged Carl Lewis early in his track and field career that he was well equipped for the long jump. He was very fast and had extraordinary spring in his legs. Numerous friends and teammates along the way, whom he trusted, provided guidance regarding conditioning, technique, and diet. A Mighty Man is a man who learns how to take counsel and heed advice from others. Solomon, in all his wisdom, put it this way: "Plans fail for lack of counsel, but with many advisors, they succeed" (Proverbs 15:22).

Let me give a word of caution here as well. People are not always right. Many people told Henry Ford that making an inexpensive car was not possible. He studied the use of assembly line mode of production as a means of producing a product at a lower price. He applied this innovated repetitive labor to the production of cars. The Model T Ford was the first car manufactured using the assembly line process and revolutionized the industry. Other car makers had to follow suit, making cars affordable for the average person. Henry Ford followed his God-given wisdom. Others will offer us advice, but they should not have the last word.

Finally, we should listen to our coaches.

Ideally, there are two sets of coaches in our lives. First, there are the parents God gave us to provide guidance in the early, formative years. The Bible says, "Train up a child in the way he should go, and when he is old he will not turn from it" (Proverbs 22:6). The word "train" in Hebrew contains within it the understanding that a parent can discern the natural tendencies and affinities of their children as they observe their talents and gifts. In an "ideal" home, it is the father's responsibility to begin guiding and lovingly directing his son or daughter in a course of life that best enables them to develop their God-given talents and abilities.

In an ideal home, parents love their children and are there for them when everyone else turns away. When parents give guidance or a word of advice to a child, they do so with a desire to serve their child. A wise child never stops listening to his parents' counsel. Please note that I qualified the above with the word "ideal." I make that distinction because we now live in a world where many children are deprived of parents who dedicate themselves to assisting them as they mature. In such cases, we still have a Heavenly Father who is always available to us if we seek Him.

There is also one other coach I want to mention. Using the athletic analogy once again, take a guess who is the Head Coach of every Mighty Man? Coach Jesus.

I don't want to trivialize our Lord by appearing to make Him too human, but that's how I related to Him when I was 18 years old. When I decided that I wanted to play college football, everyone, including most of my high school coaches, told me I couldn't. They said I was too small to play my position (offensive center) at the college level. Everyone said that the scholarships were for more gifted and physically endowed athletes. But I was determined to play college football.

Galena Park High School was legendary in Texas athletics as a pipeline for college athletes. When the scholarships came, 21 players on our football team got offers to go to the next level. Several went to major universities while others received offers to play in what was referred to as small colleges or junior colleges. The only scholarship interest in me came from Oklahoma State University in far northeast Oklahoma. I was too much of a mama's boy to travel that far from home. One of the coaches at Stephen F. Austin State University also expressed interest in me, but not enough to offer a scholarship. I decided to write him a letter making the case that if he gave me a chance, I'd make his squad. He was impressed and invited me to come to the campus for a formal visit. I got a one-year trial scholarship and made the most of it. By the start of my sophomore season, I was the first team offensive center on what became one of the greatest offensive units in SFASU history. I remained on a full scholarship through the end of my junior year. God had another purpose in my Life. I resigned the football team and enrolled at Houston Baptist University to prepare for my calling to the ministry.

Every summer, before reporting to various colleges where we played football, several former teammates and older athletes from Galena Park gathered at the high school stadium for afternoon workouts. We encouraged and challenged each other. But when the others went home, I would bow my head and say, "Okay, Coach Jesus, are You through with me yet?" And every time, "Coach Jesus" would impress upon my heart, "No, you need to run another mile or two." And every time my flesh would cry out, "But I'm tired." Then Coach Jesus would remind me, "You can do ALL things through My strength" (Phil. 4:13). Finally, I'd say, "okay, strengthen me, Coach Jesus." By the end of the summer when we reported for two-a-day workouts at SFA, I'd be in the best shape of any of the linemen and most of the backs. I'm certainly not bragging here, because it sure wasn't my idea to beat myself up with more exercise after the workouts. Still, I could listen to "Coach Jesus" or not.

Every man has an opportunity to be guided by the Ultimate Coach. He is patiently waiting for us to call upon Him, but He will never compromise on His workout schedule for us. More importantly, He will never force us to follow His coaching. It is entirely voluntary. Scripture says in James 4:2 that "...you do not have because you do not ask." The will of God is not hidden from those who sincerely want to know it. The prophet Jeremiah reminds us that finding God is never an accident: "You will seek me and find me when you seek me with all your heart" (Jer. 29:13).

Many of us are so busy with our agendas that we dare not allow God to be in charge, lest He demands we make changes. We'd rather do our own thing and then pray for God to bless it. God has something wonderful in store for us, but we will never receive it until we seek Him with our whole heart. The secret to success is to check in with the One who knows the game inside and out, including how to win. Seek the Head Coach, and then respond with total obedience.

Jesus was coaching His disciples when He said these words, "What I see the Father doing, that I do. What I hear the Father saying, that I say" (John 5:19). We cannot know what the Father is doing or what He is saying if we are not spending time alone with Him.

Securing a Launch Point

Returning to Carl Lewis and the long jump, what if, on his record-setting jump in 1996, Carl Lewis had launched the takeoff just one inch beyond the start point? The white flag of success would never have come up. Instead of setting a record, Carl Lewis would have heard the official say, "No jump. Foul. Scratch." And Lewis would have been a forgotten ex-champion.

To end right, you must start right, and the launch point for a successful life is making sure your relationship with God is secure. No one is born on the road to Heaven. Getting on the path of life eternal with God in Heaven begins with a change of course in your life. I often hear people say, "I've always been a Christian." That is impossible. As sweet and innocent as a newborn baby is, we all have one thing in common: We are all born with a sin nature that condemns us and separates us from God.

While that may sound harsh and cruel, it's not hard to see if you're willing to be honest. Just consider the facts.

Fact number 1: You never have to teach a young child how to do wrong.

You have to teach them to do what's right. That's because the sin propensity is within each child's nature: "For all have sinned and fallen short of the glory of God" (Romans 3:23KJV).

Fact number 2: You must be born again to obtain eternal life.

Jesus, while speaking to Nicodemus, a genuinely nice and good man, said, "Very truly I tell you, no one can see the kingdom of God unless they are born again" (John 3:2). Nicodemus was shocked to hear this statement, and in turn asked Jesus, "How can a grown man be born the second time?" Jesus replied, "Very truly I tell you, no one can enter the kingdom of God unless they are born of water and the Spirit" (John 3:5).

Fact number 3: God loves sinners.

Everyone must start their spiritual journey with a new birth experience, because we are all born as sinners, the first time. "But God demonstrates his own love for us in this: While we were still sinners, Christ died for us" (Romans 5:8).

Fact number 4: We are saved by grace, alone.

"For it is by grace you have been saved, through faith—and this is not from yourselves, it is the gift of God— not by works, so that no one can boast. For we are God's handiwork, created in Christ Jesus to do good works, which God prepared in advance for us to do" (Ephesians 2:8-9). Grace, simply defined, is unmerited favor. I have often told people that if good works could save a man, Heaven would be just like Earth; filled with egomaniacs strutting around and bragging about all the good things they had done to get into Heaven.

Heaven will be nothing like Earth. Instead, everyone will be humbly and joyfully pointing to Jesus and saying, "It's all because of Him. That's why we're here!"

Have you come to a place in your life where you genuinely trusted Jesus, and Him alone, to save you from your sins? If not, why not now? Simply pray:

Dear Father in Heaven, I have sinned. I believe that your Son, Jesus, died on the cross for my sins and on the third day He arose from the grave. I choose this day to turn from my sins and trust Jesus alone for my salvation. With your help, I choose this day to live the rest of my life in devotion and surrender to your will for my life. In Jesus' Name, I pray. Amen.

If you just prayed that prayer, you are ready to start living a successful life. You're ready for the next key! There can be no lasting success without discipline and integrity. Be encouraged because God promises that we can be confident of this very thing: "He who began a good work in you will be faithful to complete it" (Philippians 1:6).

I'm a big fan of the Rocky movie franchise. As soon as the sixth installment, Creed, was released, I took my grown son to see it. I have seen them all more times than I want to admit. I like them because Rocky always wins. Even when he loses, he wins. That's the way it is with Mighty Men, too. I was jogging one day and listening to a tape my children gave me that included the soundtrack of *Rocky III*, including "Eye of the Tiger." As the music got faster and faster, I started running faster and faster. I almost ran myself to death.

The 'Rocky' Road to Success

I love the movie, *Rocky III*. In it, Rocky's manager schedules another big fight with a newcomer, Clubber Lang, who destroyed every challenger he faced as he worked his way up to a title fight. But, while the challenger, Clubber Lang, is in the gym sweating it out and getting ready for their bout, Rocky is signing autographs and posing for photographs. Rocky looked like he was training but he wasn't. When the big event came, he got "Clubber Langed."

Many Christians are like Rocky in that movie. They talk a good game and appear to be real, but in truth are living a lie. We can't achieve success in life, and we'll never be Mighty Men until we are the same in private as we are in public. At our core, we must be people of deep integrity if we want to succeed, and that requires discipline and dependence on our Lord.

Webster's defines integrity as "the quality or state of being complete ... wholeness ... of sound moral principle, uprightness, honesty, and sincerity."

Reputation has to do with what people think about us, while

integrity is about who we truly are in any circumstance. God is not impressed with our reputation, but rather who we are when no one is looking but Him. God demonstrates this truth clearly in the Old Testament book of Job.

Most scholars believe that Job is the oldest book in the Bible, predating the writing of Genesis. In the first two chapters, we are given a glimpse into the mind of God and the kind of man God honors:

> …One day the angels came to present themselves before the Lord, and Satan also came with them. The Lord said to Satan, "Where have you come from?"
>
> Satan answered the Lord, "From roaming throughout the earth, going back and forth on it."
>
> Then the Lord said to Satan, "Have you considered my servant Job? There is no one on earth like him; he is blameless and upright, a man who fears God and shuns evil."
>
> "Does Job fear God for nothing?" Satan replied. "Have you not put a hedge around him and his household and everything he has? You have blessed the work of his hands so that his flocks and herds are spread throughout the land. But now stretch out your hand and strike everything he has, and he will surely curse you to your face."
>
> The Lord said to Satan, "Very well, then, everything he has is in your power, but on the man himself do not lay a finger."
>
> Then Satan went out from the presence of the Lord.

We live in the shortcut generation. We live in the generation that will spend weeks developing mottoes and logos but ignore the message and content required for success in the long term. Job was the exception to the rule. God reminded Satan that Job feared only God Almighty, shunned evil and lived uprightly. Job was, in a word, blameless! That makes him the first "Mighty Man!" I will say much more about Job in a later chapter.

Success requires discipline and dependence on God. The author of Hebrews writes, "Let us throw off everything that hinders and the sin that so easily entangles us" (Hebrews 12:1-2). We need to live the same in private as we do in public.

We must also stay focused. Carl Lewis did not run down that track looking to see if his girlfriend was in the stands. And the sprinter who breaks the world record isn't looking at the competition while he runs. He has his eyes fastened on the finish line. Many people do not succeed in life because they do not stay focused.

Taming the Lions

Have you ever wondered why a lion tamer carries a stool into a cage of lions? Common sense would tell us that it is to beat the lions over the head should they attack. However, that's not the reason. Lions are the most focused hunters on earth. A lion will lie in the brush for hours watching his prey. And when it is finally time to attack, he steals across the ground and strikes the deathblow. Lions do not take their eyes off their prey until they've accomplished their task. Lion tamers have discovered that if they walk into a cage of lions with a chair and four legs, it distracts the lion because he doesn't know which leg to focus on and it renders him almost powerless.

Focus

Have you ever been to the kitchen to get something and forgot why you entered the kitchen when you got there? Have you ever called someone, and when they answered the phone, you couldn't remember whom you called? Why is it that a football team can manage to gain only 30 yards in the first quarter and 13 minutes, but in the final two minutes of the half charge up and down the field as if the opponents had left the area? It's because the whole team becomes focused.

Most business owners get more work done on the last day before they leave for two weeks of vacation than the two weeks preceding. This is because they get focused, knowing they will be out for a while and that certain things must be done for their business to thrive. There's a law in business that says if we have one letter to write all day we will fool around and have to rush at the end of the day to write the letter. But if we have 20 letters to write, we'll get them all done. It takes focus.

What or who should we focus on? The Bible says, "Let us fix our eyes on Jesus" (Hebrews 12:2). We should be focused on the Person who has a purpose for our lives.

Passion

The next key to achieving success in life is passion. The Apostle Mark says we are to, "Love the Lord your God with all your heart and with all your soul and with all your mind and with all your strength" (Mark 12:30).

When God instructs us to love Him with all our soul, He is speaking of the seat of our emotions or passions.

Intelligence

Scripture says we are to love God with all our mind. That means intellectually. No great athlete became great without first becoming intelligent about his sport. For instance, pro golfers know every mechanical detail of their swing. They have to be totally educated in their craft. Carl Lewis became an expert about the mechanics of the long jump, perfecting his craft by knowing every detail of what transpires physically before, during, and after a long jump.

Many of us want to be successful in life, but we are not willing to take the time to study our craft. There is a price to be paid educationally. It can be said again; there are few things sadder than a man with unfulfilled potential at the end of his life. God wants us to be successful in life. To do so, we must love the Lord our God with all our mind.

Strength

Finally, the Scriptures say we are to love God with all our strength. I believe that means we also must pay the price physically. Taking care of yourself may seem like a full-time job. Neglecting that "job" though can harm your confidence, relationships, and enjoyment of life. It is important to take care of yourself as it ensures a happier and healthier life. Start on the inside with a good attitude toward life. Eat healthy foods such as fruits and vegetables. Find time to exercise. Whether it's a daily walk with the dog around the block or a gym workout, fit some exercise into each day. Take the stairs instead of the elevator, get off the bus a few stops earlier and walk the rest of the way to work, or add walking time to your lunch hour. Whatever your preference, just find ways to fit in good movement that helps keep you toned and fit. I have seen many great people fall 20 years before their time because they did not take care of themselves physically.

Lesson from a Pizza Joint

One more thing about success: We should be enthusiastic about everything we do, but especially our work. I get so tired of being around people who do not want to do what they have to do in life. I don't want a barber who does not want to be a barber. I don't want a mechanic who does not want to be a mechanic. I don't want a pastor who does not want to be a pastor. Whatever we do, we should do it all the way. If God calls us to sweep floors, we should sweep floors with all our heart. The Bible says, "Whatever you do, in word or deed, do it all to the glory of God" (Colossians 3:17).

There is a pizza chain called CiCi's Pizza that could give us all a lesson in enthusiasm. When someone walks through the door, every employee shouts, "Welcome to Cici"s Pizza!" When you leave they shout, "Goodbye, thank you for coming!" Frankly, we could all learn a lot about being enthusiastic from the minimum wage earners that make going to Cici's Pizza an enjoyable place to eat!

How can we be similarly enthusiastic? First, the right attitude is essential. Henry Ford said, "Whether you think you can or think you can't, you're right." Can you imagine what Carl Lewis thought as he started that last jump just to qualify for the finals in the most important contest of his life? He's rocking, fixing to sprint, and what if he said to himself, "Wait a minute. I'm 35 years old. Millions of people are watching me. I've got gray hair! I can't do this."

With that attitude, I don't think he could have done it. What about Michelangelo? He built scaffolding to paint upside down. I wonder how many people told him he was a fool for doing that? If he had listened to the critics, he would have instead painted the floor, and it would all be wiped away from shuffling feet. If we think we can or if we think we can't, we're right. A positive attitude is essential. Proverbs 23:7 says: "As a man thinks in his heart, so he is."

Perform

Finally, we have to perform. There is a whole industry now called Sports Psychology. Sports psychologists work with athletes to help figure out why they can't throw a curve ball or why they're in a slump. The profession was wonderfully satirized in the Robert Redford baseball movie The Natural, in which the team shrink calls losing "a disease." Now imagine this with me. There is Carl Lewis. He has his personal psychologist telling him how to jump 28 feet. He's got slogans everywhere. His mind is saying, "I can do this, I can do this." But when he gets on the starting line and is ready to go, he says to himself, "I can visualize this; I see it in my mind." Then turning to sports announcer Brent Musberger, he says, "I've already seen myself get the gold medal." Though full of confidence, he never bothers making the jump, thus never wins the medal. Visualizing success may be helpful, but finally, we have to perform.

There are a lot of people with great ideas and plans who never get around to doing them. How many times do we find ourselves driving home and thinking, "I'm going to drop a thank you note in the mail to that person who is such a blessing to me. I'm going to tell them in a letter how much I love them." We feel so good going home because we've decided to do something, but then we never get around to sending the note. Technology pioneer and Chuck E. Cheese founder Nolan Bushnell put it this way: "Everyone who's ever taken a shower has an idea. It's the person who gets out of the shower, dries off and does something about it who makes a difference."

Falling Forward

The Apostle Paul writes, "I have fought the good fight, I have finished the race, I have kept the faith. Now there is in store for me the crown...." (2 Timothy 4:7-8).

We can learn a lot from Carl Lewis if we examine his career closely. **First, we should perform as long as we can with excellence.** Many people said, "Carl, don't try it another time." But he knew deep inside that he could still compete at a high level.

The day may come when our physical abilities diminish, but until they do, we should press on for the glory of God. You will know when its time to quit.

When our bodies no longer function as they once did, we can still do the most important work of all, prayer. Not everyone can run with Olympic speed. Not everyone can sing like Brad Paisley. But all of us can pray, and nothing surpasses that in the potential for good. Isn't it just like God to reserve the highest privilege for everyone, even the oldest and least able?

The second thing we can learn from Carl Lewis is that when we fall, we should fall forward. Carl Lewis extended as long as he could, then his body would begin to contract right before he hit the sand at the end of his jump, so that his body was in a tiny ball. With this technique, his tailbone would hit as far forward as possible. Then he immediately made sure that every part of his body propelled forward so that his landing was as far forward as possible.

Learn from Carl Lewis' technique: Fall forward and continue to face forward! Jesus tells us that, "He who puts his hand to the plow and looks back is not fit for service in the Kingdom of God" (Luke 1:62).

The third thing we can learn from Carl Lewis is to get out of the pit before we celebrate. Only after he was out of the pit did he allow himself to enjoy his accomplishment. He waited until he got out of the pit lest he did something to move the marker back. There comes a time when we have to get out of the way and let the next generation do it. At least, the physical part.

Know when to quit. Do not ruin many years of good work by hanging on too long. We must also recognize the special calling that God places on the older generation to pass on what He's taught us to those who are younger, "That the generation to come might know, even the children yet to be born, that they will arise and tell their own children, that they should put their confidence in God and be obedient to Him" (Psalm 78:6-7a). It is our privilege and responsibility to "...inspire them to fear Him, so that they will never turn away from Him" (Jeremiah 32:40).

Life does not have to be mundane or laborious. I believe God wants us to enjoy our lives. Whatever we choose to do in life, we should do it with all our hearts. Paul says, "Whatever you do in word or deed, do all to the glory of God" (Colossians 3:17). Mighty Men do whatever they do in word or in deed, all to the glory of God.

Now we'll proceed to discover how to be Mighty Men with families and careers.

Chapter Two

HOW TO STAY MARRIED AND LOVE YOUR WIFE

"The Marathon"

In 1998, 12,000 runners lined up in Hopkinton, Massachusetts to run the famed Boston Marathon. They all had one thing in common — they wore yellow tags called Champion Chips.

That year, runners passed through 11 checkpoints to track their identification and time. You may wonder why the race committee was going to such lengths to monitor each athlete. Here's why.

Since the Marathon was first convened in Boston, many entrants have attempted to cheat by not running the whole race. In 1980, one such runner, Rosie Ruiz, wanted to get her name in the record books. Well, she did, in a way. When she crossed the finish line, crowds cheered, and cameras flashed. She was the first woman to finish. However, it didn't take long for someone to notice that upon receiving her prize, she wasn't perspiring like the other athletes. Although she had taken off with the group and finished with a couple of them, she had traveled in the middle—via subway.

After the Ruiz fiasco, the Marathon committee set up three checkpoints to discourage cheating. However, in 1997, runners John Murphy and Suzanne Murphy were able to start with the group, check in at all three checkpoints and cross the finish line to win their age divisions. But they didn't run the entire race.

It's still undetermined whether they enlisted other runners to run for them between checkpoints or if they jumped in and out of the contest. But somehow, they avoided running the whole race and came back in, just in time, to win the prize. In 1998, a stiffer action was taken to prevent cheating.

The Marital Marathon

Marathons have a lot in common with marriage. In fact, many marriages mirror Rosie Ruiz's story. They start out so well, and some may even seem to end okay, but if we look at the middle, we often find that they were cheating all the way.

I once heard a preacher say during a message on the family, "I've never considered divorce.... Murder, yes; but never divorce." Everyone laughed because everyone in the building knew that a preacher in his denomination had a better chance of his ministry surviving murder than a divorce.

If you're going to stay married, there is only one way to do that successfully. You must play by the rules, and God's rules do not change with the whims of men. The Supreme Court of the United States, on June 26, 2015, in the *Obergefeld* decision, reversed the laws of every state in the union, and in effect said, "God, your laws regarding marriage are antiquated and out of touch with modern society and are therefore no longer applicable to America."

But reader, when it comes to marriage, man doesn't get a vote. If you want to enjoy a life-long marriage and discover the joys that God promises those who follow Him, then it is essential that you obey His laws, despite what the culture says or does.

An Age of Disloyalty

We are living in a time when society is breaking down around us. Corporate America is no longer loyal to its employees. Likewise, employees are no longer loyal to their employers. When you land a job, you must understand that it's probably not permanent because the company can hire a younger employee for less money. It happens all the time.

Years ago, things were different. At age 16, my father went to work at Sheffield Steel, which was later bought out by Armco Steel Works. He was fresh off the farm in the mid-1940s. He then left for two years to serve his country as a soldier during the Korean Conflict. After completing his service, he came back to the steel mill, where he worked for a total of 37 years. It was once common in America to meet someone who started with a company when they were young and who stayed with that company for their entire working career. Today, such opportunities are exceedingly rare.

Loyalty in families is not a given in our society today either. The smallest but most important unit in our society is the family. When families fail, every other institution is weakened and eventually fails as well. Since biblical times, the family has been the nucleus of society, and yet it is under attack as in no other era in American or world history.

Unleashing the Power

In 1905, scientists began to understand the enormous, pent-up energy in an atom. An atom is capable of generating enough energy and electricity to light up a large building, and yet it can also generate enough power to blow up a city.

The nuclear family has similar, powerful capacities. Locked in the small group of people known as the family is the potential for great wonder and hope. At the same time, this little unit has the potential for enormous psychological, and physical harm. The most violent place in America is behind the locked doors of homes where family members are mistreated and violated every day, often perpetuating a cycle of abuse.

In It for the Long Haul

If we want to restore our nation to a place of strength and honor and build churches that make an impact, we need to start training men to understand loyalty and commitment to themselves, their wives and their children. We must find and encourage Mighty Men. It is sheer hypocrisy for men to demand from others that which they are not willing to do themselves.

God initiated the first marriage. Genesis 2:18-24 says:

The Lord God said, 'It is not suitable for The man to be alone. I will make a helper for him.' Now the Lord God had formed out of the ground all the beasts of the field and all the birds of the air. He brought them to the man to see what he would name them; and whatever the man called each living creature, that was its name... but for Adam, no suitable helper was found. So the Lord God caused man to fall into a deep sleep; and while he was sleeping, he took one of the man's ribs and closed up the place with flesh. Then the Lord God made a woman from the rib...and they will become one flesh."

Marriage is in serious trouble today. Hollywood and the media often paint any man who wants to be married for life to the same woman as a fool or a loser.

A generation ago, with the introduction of no-fault divorce, the Pill, and a predatory, porn-saturated culture, marriage became disposable. The false promise of Woodstock's "free love" became a siren song for unfaithfulness. The consequences have been nothing short of disastrous. Up to half of the children in our country, today have never lived with their dads. Fatherless homes are the single biggest contributing factor to poverty and all its harmful side effects, from welfare dependency to crime. With the media culture bombarding men with the message that they need not follow God's rules, the temptation to cheat is rampant. It takes a Mighty Man to stay faithful in all ways to his wife. The good news is that staying faithful is quite doable with God's help.

God Perceived a Problem

Let's examine God's purpose for marriage. God perceived a problem with man in his newly created world. In the Garden of Eden, man had God above him and animals beneath him, but man had no human companion with him. So God performed the very first surgical procedure, putting Adam into a deep sleep and removing a rib. The bone was not from his head which might have implied that the wife was smarter than her husband, nor from his heel giving rise to the assumption that the husband was superior to his wife. Rather, by God's design, it came from his rib cage to remind them both that they're a team of equals, mutually submissive to one another (Ephesians 5:21). God is the source of all wisdom. He intended husband and wife to be co-equal, to walk hand in hand and shoulder to shoulder, negotiating the difficulties of life in different but complimentary roles.

Next, we read that a man is to leave his parents. The Bible did not say, "for this cause shall a woman leave her parents," but rather it says that a man should leave his. A woman must leave her familiar surroundings to join and support her husband as he pursues his career when they exchange vows and get married. The wife makes the greater sacrifice, taking her husband's name, and at best, relegating her family name to a middle name, if it remains at all. The real difficulty is for a man to make the break from his parents. If men aren't careful, they can ruin their relationship with their wives by constantly comparing them to the greatest woman they have ever known—their mother. For this reason, the Bible is clear in saying, "the man shall leave his father and his mother."

Once a marriage is consummated, there should never be any doubt where the man's allegiance lies. The man's loyalty and commitment, should a controversy arise, must be for his wife, not his parents. This in no way diminishes his commitment to honor his parents. I believe that children were God's plan for providing the necessities of life for their elderly parents when a need arises. Previous generations have tried to give that responsibility away to the government, which has been more than willing to step in, but they did so at a significant cost. Our nation is now drowning in a sea of red ink that is undermining our entire economy and threatening America's national security. And who would argue that our families are better off? God's command to honor our parents is non-negotiable, but the wife should never have to wonder where the husband's first loyalty lay.

The wellbeing and security of your wife must be your priority as the head of your family. God meant for the man to leave his parents, cleave to his wife, and weave a family. Mighty Men know so, regardless of what the government does or what the culture says.

God Provided a Solution

One of the greatest passages concerning how a family should operate is tucked away in the fourth chapter of Ecclesiastes. God never intended for man's best friend to be a dog, or a hunting or drinking buddy. God intended for man's best friend to be his wife. How can she be his best friend if he does not share the intimacies of his life and withholds his deepest secrets? God intended for husbands and wives to be best friends and soulmates as well as lovers.

He designed this relationship because man and woman complement one another. When I first got married, I understood that my new bride and I were to become one flesh. Many men can't wait to be one flesh.

But right after the honeymoon, things get complicated. When they go grocery shopping and have to purchase that first tube of toothpaste, they're faced with the dilemma of deciding which brand to buy...his or hers? What about ketchup—Heinz or Hunt's? What about bread? Whole wheat or white?

Marriages seldom fail because of major issues such as sex or money, but rather a myriad of smaller and more routine disagreements that aren't dealt with according to God's pattern of tenderness and forgiveness. In fact, the Bible says little foxes spoil the vineyard (Song of Solomon 2:15). Amazingly, many men and women are driven to marriage by sexual urgency described in Paul's letter to Corinth, where he bluntly stated, "It's better to marry than to burn." (1 Corinthians 7:9) Soon after the marriage is consummated, they discover that there is a whole lot more to it than sex.

God also reminds us that there is strength in numbers. Ecclesiastes 4:9 says, "Two are better than one." I discovered early on how much wisdom God could provide me through my wife. She sees life from an entirely different perspective. The worst thing a couple can do is compete for supremacy. Men and women are different and possess unique personalities and unique gifts. In the womb of our mothers, God designed the genetic material to make an individual what he or she becomes. Wise husbands and wives embrace one another in their uniqueness rather than trying to change one another. Learn how to accept your wife as she is and thank God for her unique qualities and trust God who loves you both.

A sure way to damage a marriage is to hammer away at your spouse every time she seems to err in your eyes. Constantly remind yourself that God can handle every difficulty you face in your marriage. God is able and ready to turn every problem you face in your marriage into a miracle of grace from which your faith can be strengthened. Learn to direct every critical thought into prayer instead of always trying to "fix" your spouse. Prayer releases enough grace and patience to allow God time to work.

Marriage is a gift from God. Most Americans still get married because they recognize they need someone. Your wife completes you. "Two are better than one because they have a good return for their labor" (Ecclesiastes 4:9).

Men, we are commanded to love our wives. Though most couples know they need to love each other, many act as if they don't know they're also supposed to like one another. I meet men every day who have never developed a real friendship with their wife. Too often if one spouse tires of the other, they are done with the relationship. On the other end of the spectrum, I meet far too many older men who have remained married for years and yet act as though they hated every moment of it. They'll boast about how long they've stayed together, yet, it's very apparent they missed out on having a friendship with their wife. How sad it is to meet a man who has lived their whole adult life in a marriage with someone they never truly liked. The real joy in marriage comes when a man realizes that he shares a house with a woman who is also his best friend. Tommye and I have been married since December 27, 1970. She is without question the best friend I have ever known and continues to be the love of my life.

Men and Women Were Designed to Compliment One Another

A husband and wife are to complement each other, especially when they also like one another. I have learned in 45-plus years of marriage that when I'm at my lowest, God will lift me up through my wife, who can encourage me like no one else on the planet. Likewise, I have learned how to be sensitive when she is at her lowest ebb, and I know how to pick her up. Friendships grow on this foundation, and that builds strength that enables a marriage to last.

The Bible says, "But pity the man who falls who has no one to help him up. And also if two lie down they will keep each other warm" (Ecclesiastes 4:10-11). A married couple should comfort, console, and empower one another.

I could not have survived the death of our beloved Kathryn without Tommye. I'm certain of that. Someone may piously respond, "What about God?" Yes, He brought us both through. No question about that. But Tommye held me, and I held her through many very dark periods as we clung to the promises of God together. And after many long and lonely nights, the sun began to shine in our home once again. God showed me during those difficult days how wise and loving He was when He conceived of lifelong marriage. As always,

His purpose in holding us to the standard of life-long marriage was for our good. God hates divorce, because He loves us.

We also see in this same text that though one person can be overpowered, two can more readily defend themselves. An old song lyric, famous in the '60s, says, "You and me against the world." It is true. I pity men who have never learned how to share the intimate details of their lives with their wives. In Matthew 18:20, God did not say that if 20 or 30 are gathered together, I will be in the midst of them. Rather He said that if two or three of you are gathered together, I will be there. In verse 19, He stated that "if two shall agree on earth touching anything they shall ask, it will be done of our Father who is in heaven." Tommye and I are prayer partners, and we have seen God move in our family mightily and often. God has reduced the number of prayer partners required for miracles to happen to only two. Satan is bent on our destruction, but God says if two shall agree—if two shall walk together in a friendship and learn how to seek My face in a relationship, what you pray for will be done by your Father in Heaven. WOW… Mighty Men get that!

What a gift from God marriage is to those who understand that when marriage is honored and cherished, it stands above all other human relationships. But there's more; so much more!

In Ecclesiastes 4:12, we read, "A cord of three strands is not easily broken." Suddenly the numbers have changed. We've just been reading, two, two, and two, and now we see a reference to three. Most theologians believe that the third strand is no less than God Himself. However, I would like to offer an alternative viewpoint.

I believe the reference to three might also be speaking of reproduction. If my theory is correct, in this verse God introduces the child—a cord of three strands is not easily broken. A family is the strongest unit known to man. In simpler times, when life was much harder, there were strong, vibrant families that conquered worlds. Now, with all the creature comforts and government handouts, and assistance available, the family is disintegrating.

God's Purpose for Marriage

We have examined how God perceived a problem and how God provided a solution. Now we'll look at God's purpose for marriage. It should be obvious that if we don't know God's purpose for marriage, we'll never know when we've achieved it. I believe God's purpose for marriage is three-fold and progressive in nature. I was taught these precepts while attending seminary. Rev. Paul Burleson was our pastor during those years. He conducted a men's seminar which contained much of what I am about to share with you. The following principles helped shape my marriage and childrearing.

When a couple comes to me wanting to be married, I often have an uncontrollable urge to call in Johnny Cash to perform the song "Jackson," which begins, "We got married in a fever, hotter than a pepper sprout!" It is clear that some couples just have to be married right away. But before I agree to perform a wedding, I insist that they seriously consider what they're getting into, because God considers marriage a vow for life, not a temporary cure for passion. In fact, the Bible says it is better not to vow a vow than to vow and not pay (Ecclesiastes 5:5). Therefore, I always urge caution and require them to sit through several sessions of instruction. I always include the three-fold purpose of marriage with them:

The initial purpose: to learn how to love someone of the opposite sex.

One may ask, why would anyone get married if they did not love the other person? Let me explain. Anyone who has been married for 20 or more years would likely agree that when they got married, they didn't even begin to understand what love is. Love is giving, not getting. Relationships do not last for long if both parties are not receiving something from the relationship. Most men, in the infancy of their marriage, want the woman to meet their needs. But, according to Scripture, love has nothing to do with getting your needs met, but rather with you meeting your wife's needs. We can see this in

God's great love toward us. "For God so loved the world, that He gave His only begotten son ...." (John 3:16). The Greek language contains several words for love. Three are often cited:

Eros - erotic love

Phileo -brotherly love

Agape - unselfish, giving love

In the passage, "For God so **loved** the world that He gave His only begotten Son" (John 3:16), the Greek word "*agape*" is used. We see it again in the verse that says, "God commended His **love** toward us in that while we were still sinners Christ died for us" (Romans 5:8). In a new marriage, Mighty Men quickly understand that the relationship is not going to work if they don't give themselves entirely to it. The initial purpose of marriage is to learn to love. Our relationship with our spouse mirrors Christ's relationship to the church. We are to reflect that kind of love toward our wives, unselfishly. Developing this takes longer for some than for others, but you must learn to love like that if you want your marriage to last a lifetime.

The intermediate purpose: to rear children.

A young couple will see the birth of their first child as a rapturous gift from God. They marvel at how good God is. But they soon discover that God gave them something more complex than a new toy. He gave them a lifelong commitment. A mother cannot birth a baby unless she is willing to go to the threshold of death to do so. In spite of all the advances of modern medicine, the mother still faces enormous personal pain in bearing a child. In fact, the cost is so great that a growing number of women are opting out of having children. However, the vast majority who have given birth have said that they would gladly do it again for the joy of holding their newborn in their arms after delivery.

For fathers, this intermediate purpose for marriage may seem like a plan for wrecking their fun. With a child in the picture, we must dedicate ourselves to living the Christ life for that child to see, and invest a small fortune to rear a child all the way to adulthood. The newborn child will grow up and bear the imprint of their father. God chose the name Father for Himself and sacrificed his only Son for us, demonstrating what a loving, sacrificial father is. In due time, as we follow His example, our children will be able to transfer joyfully all they know about us to their Heavenly Father.

The Power of Example

Is it any wonder so many kids hate God today, with so many fathers failing to be the dads that God intended them to be? Many children in our country have grown up without even knowing who their father is, let alone learning that it's safe to trust and rely on him. God could have settled for calling himself King, for He is. God could have decided to call himself Creator, for He is. God could have demanded to be called Lord, for He is. But, as we learn in the New Testament, He chose Father. We have an enormous responsibility to love our children in such a way that they understand the true nature of fatherhood. Then, when we begin to tell them about their Heavenly Father, they'll say, "Man, if He's anything like my Dad, I want Him." That's what it means to be a Mighty Man.

The intermediate purpose of marriage is to bear children so that God can work in our hearts to teach us humility as we learn how to die to selfish desires. Arrogant and proud Daddies will kill their families. Hateful and self-centered mothers, who forsake their children to pursue a career and a quest for things that God has never promised, will produce kids who hate God. The proof of this is all around us. Pastors are constantly coping with the results of broken homes.

Many fathers urge their wives to re-enter the workforce as soon as possible after a child is born. In some cases of financial hardship, it's by necessity, but in most cases, Mom could stay home if Dads made wiser choices concerning finances. Dads, make sure you aren't forcing your wives to be earners so that you can have more or better stuff. Children are worth infinitely more. My greatest joy in this season of life is seeing my kids and their children walk with God. My wife being home when they needed her is primarily responsible for that. And we were able to do that on a preacher's salary, by making careful and wise choices.

God gave mankind the best of all child rearing plans when He chose mothers to nurture children. No one else can do it like Mom. No one else will respond to the cry of a child like a mother. Moms, if you're reading this, please know that nothing you can achieve outside your home will surpass the joy and satisfaction of providing a nurturing and loving environment for your children. At all costs, strive to find a way to be a mother first. Your kids need that, and you will benefit from being their mother. As with the joys derived from a lifelong marriage, God was expressing His love for you when He ordained you to be a mother first.

The ultimate purpose: to glorify God.

There was a gentleman in a church I pastored who was married for more than 50 years. His wife developed dementia and became increasingly difficult for anyone to deal with except her husband, Jim. She was in the nursing home for the last eight years of his life. Jim went to that nursing home every day to feed her, visit her, bathe her and be there for her. Loving your wife does not mean parading her in a bikini to show everyone how beautiful she is when she's young and firm. Loving your bride is about a faithful commitment until she's old and gray. Through this example, others will say of you, "So that's what it means to love Jesus with all your heart." That was what I thought as I witnessed that senior gentleman in our church visiting his ailing wife every day in a nursing home. That's what Mighty Men do.

Love means commitment, even unto death. The ultimate purpose of marriage is to glorify God. We do that when arthritis attacks our joints, and we can no longer walk without a cane, and it requires courage just to get up and get dressed each day, but we do it. We glorify God when with determination we hang in there together. We show our love for God when we see other men casting their mates aside like useless rubbish, yet, we continue to love our wives and support them without wavering. That's when others will look at us and say, "So that is what God's love looks like." Mighty Men love like that.

You and I have the opportunity to have that kind of testimony IF we remain faithful to love and like our wives all the way to the end. And for those who have lived through the tragic end of a marriage and walked through the difficulties of a divorce, you can choose now to live the rest of your life in obedience to God. He is loving and forgiving, and you now have the chance to reflect His grace by the way you live the rest of your life. Divorce is not an unforgivable sin.

The Supreme Court has redefined marriage to include same-sex couples, saying, in effect, God, you're not as wise as we. This assault on marriage flows from the same lie perpetrated on Eve in the Garden of Eden. Satan succeeded because of the silence of Adam. Adam was with her when Satan said to Eve that she didn't have to listen (Genesis 3:6). She could go her way, and he is still saying that. The reason he got away with it in the garden was that hiding in the shadows, a silent Adam did not have the guts to come out and say, "we're not going to have that in this house." A Mighty Man will refuse to be silent and will not let his wife take the brunt of Satan's assault.

Fix the Family, Fix the Nation

America is in deep trouble because there are too few Mighty Men. Many are so busy pursuing their goals that there's no time left to pursue the will of God, leaving their homes without a strong man to protect the family against the wiles of the devil. That lack of commitment to their families reverberates throughout society.

The only hope for our nation is to restore the family. We must once again embrace God's standards for the family. This will happen when we submit to the Lordship of Christ, and with the help of the Holy Spirit, submit to the Scriptures. The Bible says, "Wives submit yourselves to your husbands as unto the Lord." But it also says, "Husbands love your wives as Christ loved the church" (Colossians 3:18-19).

Considering all that Christ has done for us, doing what Christ has instructed us to do is the least we can do for Him. If we love our wives as Christ loved the church, our wives will have little difficulty submitting to our leadership. When men begin to model Jesus in their homes, then their wives will want to study their Bibles, walk with God, and honor their husbands. And the children will more likely want to follow their Moms and Dads in their pursuit of God.

Marriage's success hinges on the husband. The Bible says one cannot steal the strong man's goods until first he binds the strong man (Matthew 12:29). In America today, Satan has all too often bound the strong man. Many men have handed over the spiritual reins to their wives, conceding spiritual leadership of their families. They expect their wives to take the family to church, and do the praying and the giving. Unless men return to their posts, America is lost. When men become Mighty Men, women will have little difficulty submitting to their leadership in the home.

If we want to remain happily married, we must play by the rules of the One who created the institution. We cannot be like Rosie Ruiz and cheat our way to the finish line. We must learn to both love and like our wives. We must sacrifice for the sake of rearing godly children. And, finally, we must commit to living according to God's Biblical standards, which glorifies Him. To do this, we must yield ourselves entirely to Jesus Christ.

Chapter Three

HOW TO MANAGE A FAMILY

"1600-Meter Relay"

Imagine with me that we're at the Olympics. Before us, several runners are warming up for the 1600-Meter Relay.

Those who will run first get into their starting blocks and are alert and ready. The shot sounds and they're off!

Relay races have teams of four, in which a runner covers a specified distance called a leg, carrying a small baton which the runner must successfully pass to the next runner. The 1600-Meter Relay comprises four laps around an oval 400-meter track. As the first runner comes around the final bend, he sees the second runner already in place, waiting to take the baton. As the lead runner gets closer to the handoff, the second athlete prepares to receive the baton and begins to run. When they both hit full stride, the baton is passed. As the second runner completes his leg, he smoothly passes the baton to the third runner. The crowd cheers. The relay has been close to flawless at this point. However, as the third runner comes around the bend, something goes wrong. Whether it's fatigue, stress, or the fact that he got a little distracted, he fumbles the pass to the fourth runner, dropping the baton. For this Olympic team, the race is over.

The 1600-meter relay illustrates an important truth about family life. One generation passes the baton to the next generation, and the race goes on. However, if one generation drops the baton, the race is over. Just like that, the family's good name is damaged forever.

There are many instances of Olympic teams who would have set a world record had not one of the team members mishandled the handoff. Perhaps the most dramatic illustration of this happening in the Olympics occurred during the Beijing Games in 2008 by the US team. Darvis Patton and Tyson Gay, two world class runners, both took responsibility for the dropped baton. Not only was USA men's team disqualified for dropping the baton, but within a span of thirty minutes, the heralded women's team did so as well. Both drops happened in the prelims and ended any chance of winning medals in an event the US had historically dominated.

With that in mind, now envision the 1600-meter relay team as comprising a great-grandparent handing the baton to a grandparent, who hands the baton to a parent, who in turn hands that baton to a growing child. One generation of spiritual neglect can destroy a family's legacy of godliness. Family life is certainly a challenge, and many families are not surviving.

From Post-Christian to Anti-Christian

In his 1979 book, *Whatever Happened to the Human Race*, Francis Schaeffer called America a post-Christian nation. But we are now living in an anti-Christian nation which has little patience nor tolerance for people of faith. If there is not a revival soon, it's only going to get worse.

Several years ago, a new toll road was completed around the city of Houston. Drivers who purchase an EZ Tag windshield sticker could use special lanes, driving at cruising speed past the tollbooths. A camera would read the tag number and debit an account, refreshed as needed by a credit card on file.

I was a little reticent to get my tag. Such devices are a little scary for me. However, I grew increasingly envious of other drivers who were zipping along without having to stop. I'll never forget going on a trip with several of our deacons. One of them was driving his car equipped with an EZ Tag. He kept bypassing the toll booths while

I stopped to pay tolls, and a car full of grown men taunted me by making faces as they roared by. Fortunately, God is just and loves preachers. While the deacon and his allies were making faces at me and poking fun, he missed his final exit and had to drive several extra miles out of the way, enabling me to beat him to our destination. Men are just big boys, and we tend to compete at everything. This time, I won!

The technology to track a moving vehicle traveling at high speeds and then billing the driver without any physical contact underscores the reality that we are living in the shadows of End Times Prophecy. The book of Revelation has much to say about the coming Anti-Christ who will spawn an anti-Christian civilization, which openly persecutes anyone who dares to believe and practices Christianity. Leading up to that age there will be increasing hostilities toward anything that is holy and godly. Your family is among the most hated of all because the family was instituted by God and is designed to represent Him on the earth. Your family is directly in the crosshairs of Satan.

Don't Look Back

In 1997, USA Olympian, Michael Johnson was set to run the anchor leg of the 1600-meter relay. He had already set a world record at a previous event but had strained a hamstring. It looked like he would not be able to run, and the coaches began to consider alternates. But at the last moment, the coaches decided to insert his name, because they realized that even if he were slightly injured, he'd still be better than anyone replacing him. So, running with a torn hamstring, Johnson ran the final leg, and the team walked away with a world record.

At times, managing a family is like running the relay with a torn hamstring. I often think about how nice it would be to live in a simpler era. But the reality is that we will never return to simpler times, so it's foolish to look back. A seasoned runner will tell you that great athletes never look back to see what's behind them or where the competition happens to be. If you're looking over your left shoulder, someone's likely to pass you on the right.

We have no choice but to focus on where God has planted us and depend on His strength to overcome the difficulties we face in a culture that is increasingly hostile to Christians. Just a few years ago, had a male entered the women's locker room at a high school or college campus, police would have been alerted, and the man would have been hauled off to jail for a criminal offense. Today, powerful forces are enacting laws that criminalize the act of preventing a man from entering women's restrooms and even the women's showers. The offense? Denying a gender-confused male his "civil rights." This kind of thinking is the inevitable result of abandoning reason, rational thinking, and truth itself, as we turn away from Christianity and become a society adrift in moral relativism.

In his thought-provoking work, *The Family Under Siege*, George Grant writes that "We are under siege. We cannot deny it any longer. Our families are facing a fierce and unprecedented challenge, one that may threaten their very existence. None of us is exempt from its ravages. No one can avoid its consequences. No one can afford to ignore it."

How We Got Here

William Bennett, a former cabinet member during the Reagan administration, compiled irrefutable evidence that families are in deep trouble in his book, *The Index of Leading Cultural Indicators*, published more than 30 years ago. Out-of-wedlock births were up 400%; divorce was up 400%; domestic violence was up 320%; abandoned children were up 500%, and teen suicide was up 200%. All this happened in just the previous three decades. I don't know how much these alarming statistics have risen since, but not one of them is trending in the right direction. The family is truly under siege!

Isn't it sad that after virtually every state in the union voted to reject abortion, that in 1973, a majority of the nine members of the United States Supreme Court ruled that an unborn child had no rights whatsoever and that a woman had a constitutional right to abort her baby if she chose? With the stroke of a pen, unborn children were declared to be expendable. These children were just blobs of tissue; we were told, a mass in the womb with no legal or natural rights. One argument advanced by abortion advocates was that the "procedure" would eliminate unwanted children. They also claimed that abortion would make families less violent and that teen suicide would decline because every child born would be loved. It was all a pack of lies.

When we deem ourselves wiser than God, we soon discover what fools we are. The culture of death has long ceased debating these matters because the truth is too embarrassing. Now the culture of death is turning its venom on the other end of life, promoting euthanasia. There is no persuasive argument against euthanasia if we have already established that people have a right to choose who lives and who dies. The outlook is grim, and our only hope is for God to raise up a generation of Mighty Men who will build godly families while working together to restore moral sanity to our fallen world.

What is a successful family? It's no longer the idealized suburban model epitomized by TV's "Ozzie and Harriet," which portrayed solid values. I used to enjoy the show. Back in the '50s when "Ozzie and Harriet," "Leave It to Beaver" and "Father Knows Best" were popular, some preachers said that buying a TV was little more than inviting Satan into your home. Many declared that television, which started out clean, was promoting ungodly entertainment. Now that it has become a moral sewer, the pulpit is largely silent. Millions watch the filthiest programs the world has ever seen, 24/7, with devices that allow men to access pornography anytime and anywhere they choose. Mighty Men are under siege. And apart from a revival, it will only get worse.

An Extension of God Himself

Genesis 1:1 says, "In the beginning, God created the heavens and the earth." The Hebrew word *Elohim*, is translated "God." The word is a plural noun that speaks of more than one. The Bible is clear that there is only one God, which makes this verse difficult to explain. Orthodox Christianity has reconciled this dilemma by teaching that God has revealed Himself as a triune God: God the Father, God the Son, and God the Holy Spirit. As we read through the rest of the first chapter of Genesis, we find in the 26th verse that God, in a Heavenly Council, says, "Let us make man in our image." So man was created in the image of Almighty God with a triune nature of body, soul, and spirit. Adam enjoyed his daily walk with God, but he needed more…he needed a human companion. God recognized and acknowledged that it was not good for man to be alone, and He created a woman out of a rib from Adam's side. He created man and woman to be an extension of God Himself.

An Expression of God's Nature

Man and woman were created to be an expression of God's nature. Romans 1:19 says, "What may be known about God is plain to them because God has made it plain to them." We also read in Romans 2 that the laws of God have been written upon our hearts. That explains why when we see something that is contrary to God's law, our conscience says, "that's just not right." God has written the truth of His Word on the tablets of every man's heart to prevent us from marching headlong into evil without warning. However, if we choose to disobey the inner witness of God's Spirit, our conscience becomes calloused. In time, evil becomes good and good becomes evil, as our foolish hearts are darkened. In the end, we excuse any bad behavior, including that which is most perverse and even dangerous. The Scriptures are frank about the decline of decency when man turns from God:

The wrath of God is being revealed from heaven against all the godlessness and wickedness of people, who suppress the truth by their wickedness, since what may be known about God is plain to them, because God has made it plain to them. For since the creation of the world, God's invisible qualities—his eternal power and divine nature—have been clearly seen, being understood from what has been made, so that people are without excuse.

For although they knew God, they neither glorified him as God nor gave thanks to him, but their thinking became futile and their foolish hearts were darkened. Although they claimed to be wise, they became fools and exchanged the glory of the immortal God for images made to look like a mortal human being and birds and animals and reptiles.

Therefore God gave them over in the sinful desires of their hearts to sexual impurity for the degrading of their bodies with one another. They exchanged the truth about God for a lie, and worshiped and served created things rather than the Creator—who is forever praised. Amen.

Because of this, God gave them over to shameful lusts. Even their women exchanged natural sexual relations for unnatural ones. In the same way, the men also abandoned natural relations with women and were inflamed with lust for one another. Men committed shameful acts with other men, and received in themselves the due penalty for their error.

Furthermore, just as they did not think it worthwhile to retain the knowledge of God, so God gave them over to a depraved mind, so that they do what ought not to be done. They have become filled with every kind of wickedness, evil, greed and depravity. They are full of envy, murder, strife, deceit and malice. They are gossipers, slanderers, God-haters, insolent, arrogant and boastful; they invent ways of doing evil; they disobey their parents; they have no understanding, no fidelity, no love, no mercy. Although they know God's righteous decree that those who do such things deserve death, they not only continue to do these very things but also approve of those who practice them (Romans 1:18-32).

That passage richly describes this culture. Adam and Eve were created and as an expression of God's nature, but also as an extension of God's person. In that same verse, He says, "and let them have dominion over all the earth." Adam was the only created being given such authority. Eve was created as Adam's companion, and together they were designed to be an exhibit of God's dominion. Mighty Men understand that.

In a previous chapter, I discussed how two are better than one and that a cord of three strands cannot easily be broken. I believe that God has designed families such that when a man and a woman in a marriage become one flesh, they literally join heart to heart and spirit to spirit. There is more than their combined strength in that relationship, for the Bible says, where two are gathered in my name, there I am in the midst of them (Matthew 18:20).

God placed man in the garden and gave him dominion over the earth. In His sovereignty, He designed the family to become a cohesive unit so that no matter what fears we face or what challenges come our way, with God as our partner, we can take dominion over our circumstances. When a family operates as designed, they can take dominion over the world and not just survive, but thrive. In Christ, we are more than conquerors. That means that the worst of times, can also be the best of times. Mighty Men get that.

An Example of God's Church

The family is also an example of the church. "For this reason, a man will leave his father and mother and cleave only to his wife. This is a profound mystery, but I am talking about Christ and His church" (Ephesians 5:31-32). It's as if God transitions suddenly from one subject to another. But in reality, He's announcing that the family is a picture of His church.

What is a church? A church is a gathering of "called out" people who understand who God is and who devote themselves to His kingdom. The first family, Adam and Eve, were designed to be exactly that. The most fundamental manifestation of the church occurs when we gather with our families for private worship. When a husband and wife pray together, they celebrate Jesus and His resurrected life. They are the church. The buildings in which we meet just house the church. The building is sanctified only to the degree to which we gather to pray and worship in it.

Each of our families has the same elements. Every Mighty Man is to be the high priest of his home. God has called each man to lead his family in prayer, Bible study, and worship. Have you prayed with your wife this week? Today? Mighty Men do that! We shouldn't wait to go to church to pray. We need to pray at home with our wives and children as well. If we just pray at church on Sunday, it tends to become "religious." But if we pray at home with our families when no one else is looking, true worship takes place as Jesus joins us.

Tapping Into the Greatest Power

Our families were designed to exemplify God's church. We become part of a family by birth or adoption. In healthy families, the bond remains strong no matter how bad things may become. Even if our children end up in prison, we continue to love them. That is precisely how the church should function, because the church is composed of twice-born people; sinners who are washed in the blood of the Lamb and joined by the bond of the Holy Spirit. When we teach or families how to love like that we tap into the greatest power this world has ever known. Your family becomes your Heaven on earth. Your home becomes your favorite place to be.

For that reason, Scripture says, "I show you a profound mystery, for I am speaking of the church." In an earthly family, a biological father or mother can say that their blood is in that child's veins, and there is a natural love. The church should have an even greater love because the blood of the Lamb, God's only Son, empowers it.

A child cries and demands attention when he or she is young, always demanding their way. But as that child grows and becomes mature, they become a contributing part of the family. God intended the church to be the same way. As we grow in Christ, we become givers rather than takers. We should give our time, our resources, our intellect and anything else over which we are stewards.

The Duty of Fathers

God instructed Moses to teach the Fathers to impart knowledge of God to their children. God knew that the future of Israel depended on healthy families. Deuteronomy 6 provides instructions on a Father's responsibility to his family. Like Israel, America's future depends on healthy families. Read the following verses very carefully and prayerfully.

> These are the commands, decrees and laws the Lord your God directed me to teach you to observe in the land that you are crossing the Jordan to possess, so that you, your children and their children after them may fear the Lord your God as long as you live by keeping all his decrees and commands that I give you, and so that you may enjoy long life. Hear, Israel, and be careful to obey so that it may go well with you and that you may increase greatly in a land flowing with milk and honey, just as the Lord, the God of your ancestors, promised you.
>
> Hear, O Israel: The Lord our God, the Lord is one. Love the Lord your God with all your heart and with all your soul and with all your strength. These commandments that I give you today are to be on your hearts. Impress them on your children. Talk about them when you sit at home and when

you walk along the road, when you lie down and when you get up. Tie them as symbols on your hands and bind them on your foreheads. Write them on the doorframes of your houses and on your gates (Deuteronomy 6:1-8).

Moses' instructions to the fathers are clear:

- Fear the Lord God
- Keep all the statutes and commandments
- Love the Lord God with all their heart, soul, and might.
- Educate their children with vigilance

And Moses gave the fathers instructions on how they were to educate their children. He instructed them to make spiritual and Biblical education a way of life, not an hour or two at the church house. Look carefully at verses 7-9. The fathers were to talk about God's Word and precepts when they…

- Sat in their houses
- When they were "walking by the way…"
- When they went to bed at night (Bedtime stories, prayer, etc.)
- When they rose up in the morning

Mighty Men make Christianity a lifestyle and impart spiritual truths by applying Biblical truth to the ordinary incidences that families deal with every day. Men are to look for ways to make the Bible come alive. And finally, Moses made the men of Israel a promise that if they lived a God-honoring life before their families, the day would come when they would reap a rich benefit.

Now men, get ready for this truth. I have personally witnessed the reality of the promise I am about to share with you in the lives of my children. "In the future, when your son asks you, "What is the meaning of the stipulations, decrees, and laws the Lord our God has commanded you?" tell him: "We were slaves of Pharaoh in Egypt, but the Lord brought us out of Egypt with a mighty hand" (Deuteronomy 6:20-21).

In effect, Moses said to the Fathers, "If you live your life before your family as I have instructed you to live, the day will come when your sons will ask you why? And you will have a story of your own to tell of the ways God has delivered you, with the result being children who want to embrace your faith." **That, men, is the ultimate goal of every Mighty Man.** Is that your goal?

Learn to Lean on Jesus

Now, how do we build successful families? The answer is quite simple. First, we must learn to lean on Jesus. I cannot think of a better text to underscore this than Matthew 11:28-30, which begins, "Come unto me all you who are weary and burdened." Everyone can relate to that. Is there anyone trying to build a family who cannot relate to that? The passage continues: "...and I will give you rest. Take my yoke upon you and learn from me for I am gentle and humble in heart, and you will find rest for your souls, for my yoke is easy, and my burden is light."

Learn From The Scripture

Secondly, we need to learn from the Scripture, "But as for you, continue in what you have learned and have become convinced of because you know those from whom you learned it.... All scripture is God-breathed and useful for teaching, rebuking, correcting and training in righteousness. ..." (2 Timothy 3:14,16). Those of us who want to build a successful family should ask ourselves one important question. "How much time are we spending reading and studying God's Word?" Every word of the Bible is God-breathed, and the degree to which we conform our lives to His Word is the extent to which we will be successful in building a healthy family. Lean on Jesus. Learn from His Word.

Learn to Listen

Thirdly, we must listen to others. The Bible says, "Children obey your parents" (Ephesians 6:1). Amazingly, parents get a lot smarter when a child reaches adulthood. Why? Because most children refuse to listen to their parents when they're younger, especially during the teen years.

Ephesians 5:21 says, "Submit yourself one to another in the fear of God." Only once in our marriage did I make a major decision against the council of my wife, and we both lived to regret it. I cringe when I hear about men who buy houses, change jobs or make major decisions without consulting their wives. Few people have stronger personalities than mine, and yet I've learned that I must listen to my wife if I'm to walk according to God's Word.

Fathers also must learn to hear their children. Ephesians 6:4 warns fathers "do not exasperate your children." You may have the right to demand obedience from your kids, but the wise father learns to listen. Do not ignore what they have to say. Men who refuse to listen to their children often live to regret it. If we want to build successful families, we must lean on Jesus. We must learn from His Word. And we must listen to each other.

Learn to Laugh

Fourthly, we must learn to laugh. Many men believe the lie that they should never let their hair down because to do so is to reveal weakness. How sad. Fathers, you must live your life in such a way that you create an environment in your home where the members of your family not only love and respect you, but they also like you. Don't take yourself so seriously. Every man needs to laugh at himself. Every so often you just need to pull the car over and laugh. Now and then you need to put the paper down and just laugh. Sometimes you need to realize that you're not going to make your appointment on time and just laugh. The rain will find us, but we have to look to find the rainbows.

Learn to Leave the Hurts Behind

Finally, we must learn to leave the hurts behind and not keep dredging them up. When an explosion occurs within our families, the last thing we should do is drag up something that happened six months or six years earlier. If your family members are forced to live in the bondage of always being reminded of their failures, they will find a way out of that bondage and your family will be destroyed.

Scripture reminds us that when Jesus forgives our sin, he buries it in the deepest ocean to be remembered no more. And when old sin comes back to haunt us, we can be assured that it is not coming from God, but from Satan, who is the accuser.

We must learn to like those we love. Laugh when we can. Look for the rainbows. And finally, leave the hurts behind. Our family members are just humans striving to honor God, and occasionally they'll mess up. So will you! Mighty Men learn to leave the hurts behind!

Chapter Four

HOW TO DEAL WITH CHILDREN

"The 100-Meter Sprint"

The 100-meter sprint is the star attraction in most Olympics, featuring the fastest men in the world. When a runner crouches at the starting line, he must leap into full stride when the starter's pistol is fired and sprint at top speed to the finish line.

This race takes place in less than 10 seconds for the truly proficient sprinter. In fact, it can be over in less time than it takes a spectator to introduce himself to the person in the next seat.

Likewise, children are the star attractions in every family, and rearing them is over before you know it. It seems like only yesterday that our first child was born. The next thing I knew, I was attending the high school graduation ceremony for the last child in our family. I can't fathom where the time went since our three children were born. I can still remember when Kathryn and I moved to Pearland, Texas in late spring of 1990, to assume my duties as the pastor of First Baptist Church. Tommye, and our two older children remained in Burleson, Texas, so our two older children could finish the school year at their respective schools.

Kathryn and I stayed with my mother and father, and we drove 26 miles every morning to Pearland, where she finished the school year. She was only in the sixth grade at the time. I remember that I

75

made a month-long commitment to her. For the hour it took to get there, and the time it took to get back, we wouldn't listen to the radio. Instead, she could ask any question she wanted, and I would answer it completely. That is a challenge I'd like to put to all fathers. I am not talking about the standard reply, "Because Daddy said so." I'm challenging you to take the time to answer any and every question asked by your child. You will be amazed at how fertile their minds are and how much they want to know. When the word "why" ends every sentence, it's possible to discuss intricate, detailed, philosophical questions.

The conversation goes something like this: "What is that, Daddy?" "It looks like smoke, Sweetheart." "Why is that smoke there, Daddy?" "Well, I guess someone is burning something." "Why, Daddy?" "Well, I don't know, but let's think about some of the reasons they might be burning something." The month passed like lightning. It seems like one moment we were driving back and forth to Pearland, waiting for the rest of the family to join us in our new home, and the next moment Kathryn and her siblings were grown up.

Not only did she become an adult and go off to college, but in 2004, in the early morning hours, she departed this life and went to Heaven while sleeping in our home, and left us with a broken heart. My son is married and is now the father of twins. Our oldest daughter is married with two children in college. Parents of small children need to cherish the time they have now. When in doubt, take pictures, and always hug them as often as you can because there is no assurance they will be there tomorrow. Mighty Men take time for their children.

As childhood passes with a speed akin to the 100-meter sprint, parents find themselves wondering what they can do to ensure that their children receive everything they need to become sound, happy, productive, mature adults. Many parents with grown children find themselves wondering if they did all they could and what they should be doing now.

Using the Ultimate Handbook

God's Word is our handbook for life. And, once again, He provides us with all we need to know. In Deuteronomy 6:1-2 we read, "These are the commands, decrees and laws the Lord your God directed me to teach you to observe in the land that you are crossing the Jordon to possess, so that you, your children and their children after them may fear the Lord your God as long as you live by keeping all His decrees and commands that I give you, and so that you may enjoy long life."

Stop and consider what He just said. He is getting ready to give us the secret to a long and happy life. As long as we live as He instructs us, not only will we live happy lives, but our children and their children will live long and happy lives as well. Look at what He says in His instructions to his Chosen People.

"Hear, O Israel, and be careful to obey so that it may go well with you and that you may increase greatly in the land flowing with milk and honey, just as the Lord, the God of your fathers, promised you. Hear, O Israel: The Lord our God, the Lord is One. Love the Lord your God with all your heart and with all your soul and with all your strength. These commandments that I give you today are to be upon your hearts. Impress them on your children. Talk about them when you sit at home and when you walk along the road, when you lie down and when you get up. Tie them as symbols on your hands and bind them on your foreheads. Write them on the door frames of your houses and your gates" (Deuteronomy 6:3-9).

God has given us a very direct command with a promise. We are to apply the things we have learned about our faith as we live out our lives while… "we sit in our homes, walk along the roadways of life, and when we prepare to go to bed at night." We are even instructed to wear jewelry that reflects our faith when appropriate, and to decorate our homes in such a way that those who enter know that we are followers of Christ. And if we do these things, we will prosper and enjoy a long life. My wife has worked hard to make sure that when people enter our home, they know that we're serious about our faith. Our children grew up in a home that reflected our faith.

Men, what is the greatest desire of you heart?" Is it to rear godly children who will learn to love and serve Jesus? You must be willing to subordinate all other goals to that one primary ambition. If that's not where you are, I hope to persuade you to re-evaluate your goals by the time you finish this book. My prayer is that when you finish and consider what you've read, you will seriously consider living your life wholly devoted to training your children to love God with all their hearts. How empty and sad your life will be if they reject your Lord. Mighty Men make discipling their children their top priority.

Our chief responsibility is not putting bread on the table or to protect our kids, though both are vital. Our highest calling is to model Christ to our families and mentor our children to love Him above all else. We need to show them not only how to succeed, but how to handle failure. Many of us, especially men, have grown up in a culture that has taught us never to let down our guard, to withhold our tears and refrain from showing our weaknesses. Such thinking damages our children, who need and long for parents who are real and who will nurture them to be just like Jesus.

Life Lessons from My Dad

My Dad was not a Christian until I was an adult. He didn't take us to church, which he now regrets. Fortunately, my mother was serious about getting her children to church, and my younger sister and I both heard the gospel at an early age because of her. I was saved when I was 7 years old, when my Sunday School teacher led me to Christ in our home, as my mother looked on. I will be forever grateful for a Mom who cared about my soul.

But my father did teach me values for which I will be grateful forever. He taught me the importance of keeping my word. He taught me a work ethic, as I watched him toil in a steel mill, that at its peak, employed 17,000 men and women. Some of my earliest memories include that of my dad walking home, bent over at the end of a long day at the plant. He and other men who lived in our neighborhood, less than a mile from the mill, wore a path which they plodded every afternoon. I'd listen for the whistle to blow, signifying a shift change which meant dad was soon headed home, and I'd begin looking for him. When I finally saw him on the trail, I'd run to him and joining him, walk hand in hand back to our modest house. He started his days around four in the morning and got home around three in the afternoon. He did that every day for 37 years until the plant was closed and he was forced to take early retirement.

I discovered firsthand what working at the plant was all about when I was 18, the summer after I graduated from high school. Employees' children could hire on for summer work. Jobs were given a ranking according to difficulty. The Mold Foundry, where my father was a foreman, was a five-point job that no one wanted. I applied, and to my delight, or so I thought, I got it. It was invaluable to me because I saw what my dad faced on a daily basis. I saw ladles of steel from which the molds were made. I saw how they used high-powered equipment and fine sand to shape the design over which was poured hot metal that made the mold for use in other parts of the plant. I saw men work with metals that were so hot they had to work in asbestos clothing. I breathed the foul air and went to the clinic at least once a week, like the rest of the guys, where medical staff routinely removed flakes of metal from our eyes. Safety goggles were inadequate to filter all of the particles of metal floating in the air, that while giving the appearance of glitter, in fact, presented a constant danger of permanent eye damage. There was no OSHA Representative to protect the workers in that day. Men needed the work, and accepted the risk.

It was there that my father taught me lessons about life, not so much by what he said but by what he did. He taught me about going to work when I didn't want to, sticking it out when I didn't feel like it, and always showing up on time. I still remember the respect the men in that plant showed my father because he had earned it. These lessons can't be taught in a classroom. Mighty Men understand that.

My father wasn't a Christian when I was growing up, but he taught me much that contributed to the person I am today. I never experienced fear of being abandoned, which many of my friends knew, because my parents never entertained the thought of divorce. Yes, we had some tough times, but my father did what was necessary to meet our daily needs. He went to work every day and came home every night. Though he did not lead in my spiritual development, thanks be to God, he was saved as an adult and became a truly Mighty Man to me.

I've been a fan of Pastor Chuck Swindoll for many years because he shares his life as an open book. He laughs. He cries. He tells about his successes and also his failures. Some of the greatest object lessons we will ever present to our children and their children will come as they watch how we live our lives. It is our high privilege to mentor our kids.

The Bible says in Deuteronomy 6:1, "These are the commands, the decrees, and the laws that the Lord your God directed me to teach you to observe them." The home and the church are the two places where children will learn about right and wrong. They won't hear of Biblical values from television, the movies or the music of our culture. Our opportunity to impart godly values decreases as our children get older because school and other activities will consume more and more of their time. And, everywhere they turn, those values and the things of God's Word will be undermined and discredited. That's why it is vital that we teach our children the Word when they're very young. Mighty Men do that!

Having the Right Motive

Here's another important matter-—our motivation for training our children must always be pure. It should not be simply to make them successful, or to protect them from the evils of this world, as important as that is. It can never be to protect or advance our reputation. The driving motivation of our hearts should always be to love God with all our heart, with all our mind, with all our soul, and with all our strength (re. Deuteronomy 6:5). Our "heart" is the center of our emotions. Our "soul" is the center of our conscience. Our "strength" refers to our physical body. God is saying that we are to love Him—not ourselves—with our whole being! If our kids sense that, they will learn to love Him as well. We will never obtain perfection in this life. There are no perfect parents. We'll all fail to some degree in training up our children. However, our goal must be to live a life so transparently in love with God that our children understand that we are trying to fulfill this assignment, not because we go to church, or preach, or teach, or because we're deacons or leaders, but because we sincerely love Him. Mighty Men get that!

Another important thing to remember is that children innately know when things aren't right. Eventually, they will figure out if you're going to church out of a sense of religious duty rather than devotion to Christ. Never underestimate the importance of children knowing that your church life flows out of a genuine love for the things of God, not out of love for self or man's acclaim.

Taking Every Opportunity

How are we to achieve all of this? God speaks to that in the passage we're studying. We are to impress these precepts upon our children 24/7, talking about them when we are sitting at home. When our kids were small, we knew we should have a family altar daily, and we had them off and on. I wish that I could say that we had a family altar time every day of our children's lives, but we didn't. We started them so many times I lost count. But, I believe the Scriptures teach that as important as a family altar is, there is something more important. God wants us to have the kind of lifestyle that when we sit in our homes and an opportunity arises, we will teach our children spiritual principles. When we are walking along the way with them, whether it's a stroll through the park or the zoo, or hustling through a grocery checkout, we are to stay tuned in to the Holy Spirit, and capitalize on object lessons that communicate spiritual principles.

That was our Lord's method. I can picture Jesus out on the hillside, saying, "see how that guy is scattering the seed and how the wind blows some of it away, with some settling upon the rocks and some on good soil?" He then taught His hearers profound spiritual lessons that were eternally true. I believe that often when He spoke in parables, the people standing by could visualize the lesson He was teaching because He referenced something nearby or familiar in their experience. Mighty Men seize every opportunity to impart truth to their children.

The greatest life lessons happen along the way, often by accident rather than on purpose. The worst things I taught my kids, were taught without my knowing. Things like losing my cool with someone who failed to meet my expectations while waiting on me in a restaurant. How often have I witnessed behavior in my children that I didn't like, only to be reminded by the Holy Spirit that they learned it from me!

But I rejoice to report some great successes along the way. Like the rainy, cold, day when we passed a physically challenged man trying to change a tire on the side of the road while sitting in a wheelchair. Several other motorists passed without stopping, as did I. But my conscience took effect, and I turned the car around. My children hadn't seen the man in need and wanted to know why we were stopping. Then they watched through the windows as I changed the man's tire in a cold, drizzling rain. The Bible wasn't opened, verses weren't quoted, but they witnessed a lesson in compassion.

We need to ask God to teach us to be more sensitive to such opportunities to teach the Word along the way. When we ask Him, we then find the real value of fishing or hunting trips, or even mowing the grass. Oswald Chambers says again and again in his devotional guide, *My Utmost for His Highest*, that "The bulk of your life is lived in the routine and drudgery. That is where real Christianity is experienced." We have this mistaken notion that going to church is spiritual and the rest of our lives is secular. Real Christianity is lived in everyday life giving a spiritual component to everything we do. The last thing your children should hear from you each night is your prayer and blessing for them. What a way to put a child to bed! Mighty Men do that.

Wearing Your Faith

In Deuteronomy 6:8, Moses instructed the Jews to wear jewelry containing verses to remind them of their covenant relationship with God. But long after they forsook walking with God, they continued wearing the jewelry for a show. Many Christians follow that pattern today, unfortunately.

It's entirely wholesome to wear an expression of our love for Christ in the form of jewelry, as long as we're striving to live the life the jewelry promotes. Soul winners trained in Evangelism Explosion often wear a pin with two question marks on it in hopes that someone will ask them what it means, opening the door for a presentation of the Gospel.

Other Christians wear two little feet, often leading to an opportunity to present the truth that every life is sacred, including the life of a pre-born baby. Another popular piece of jewelry contains the encryption "WWJD," representing the question, "What Would Jesus Do?" This question reminds those wearing it to examine each situation in light of how Jesus might have responded. Others wear the symbol of the fish, which was used in the First Century by persecuted Christians to signify to other believers that they were followers of Jesus. It's fine to wear such symbols, as long as our lives reflect the symbol we bear.

This same principle should apply to our homes. People should be able to sense God's presence when they enter your home. They ought to sense that the home belongs to Jesus.

In Deuteronomy, we also find a warning in verse 10 where we read, "When the Lord your God brings you into the land He swore to your fathers, to Abraham, Isaac and Jacob to give you—a land with large, flourishing cities you did not build, houses filled with all kinds of good things you did not provide, wells you did not dig, and vineyards and olive groves you did not plant—then when you eat and are satisfied, be careful that you do not forget the Lord, who brought you out of Egypt, out of the land of slavery. Fear the Lord your God, serve Him only...."

Prosperity can be a distraction.

It's often true that when times are tough, we turn to Jesus. But when everything is going well, many forget God. Instead of giving Him the first fruits, we give Him the left overs, if anything at all. Instead of rushing into His presence and thanking Him for all He's done, we forget Him and indulge ourselves. "But the worries of this life, the deceitfulness of wealth and the desires for other things come in and choke the Word, making it unfruitful" (Mark 4:19). Prosperity can be dangerous.

Comfort can cause forgetfulness.

God warns us in Deuteronomy 6:11 to be careful to avoid forgetting God, who created our wealth and blessed us with it, once we have houses full of things that God has graciously allowed us to accumulate. Who would deny that as Americans, we have been blessed above all nations? Many people living in the inner city slums would be considered wealthy in much of the rest of the world. Millions travel to America legally and illegally to have a chance to participate in the vast opportunities for wealth this free country affords. We take so much for granted. Comfort can be dangerous for godly parents if they forget who truly owns their possessions.

Years ago, I read the book *The Tempting of America* by Robert Bork, and was impressed with his understanding of our culture. Mr. Bork, who was nominated to the U.S. Supreme Court but rejected and slandered by liberals for his conservative positions, possessed a great legal mind. A law professor at Yale for more than 30 years and a former U.S. Solicitor General, he would have been an excellent member of the Supreme Court had he been confirmed. He wrote in his book that men showed more concern about whether their DVD players worked than succeeding in life. I couldn't agree more. Someone once noted that the three most pressing issues on the minds of people in church on Sunday mornings are:

1) When will the preacher finish his sermon?

2) What are we having for lunch? And,

3) What's on TV this afternoon?

No wonder God doesn't move in power in our midst like He once did. Our lukewarm faith, brought about by affluence and complacency, is far removed from the faith of men of God in the past who fell on their faces and pleaded with God to send rain because if He didn't, their families would starve.

Prosperity is a great blessing, to be sure. But when people are doing well, it is easy to forget God. The issues become superficial, such as grieving over the first scratch on our new automobile more than the people around us who are lost and going to hell.

Men are called be mentors.

The greatest calling of parenting is to mentor our children. The Bible says that parents are to fear the Lord and not follow other gods. God knows when a new bass boat means more to us than our children. Career advancement and money can become our gods. Many men defend their excessive work as helping their families when, in reality, they are only helping themselves afford more stuff. They say it's all for the children and all for the family, but it's not.

Fathers are to keep God's commands and fear the Lord, and remain faithful to rear their children to love Him. Scripture promises the faithful dad that God will in turn work in the lives of his children. "In the future...." (Deuteronomy 6:20). We often become distraught when a child strays and nothing seems to be working in our present circumstances. But the Bible says to stay faithful. There is a corollary in Proverbs 22:6 that says, "Train up a child in the way he should go, and when he is old he will not depart from it." Mighty Men understand this principle. God's promise is to work "in the future," if we remain faithful now.

Remember the story in Luke 15 about the prodigal son, raised by the perfect father? It mirrors a picture of God the Father. Despite the father's best efforts, one of the two sons had a mind to wander, and wander he did! But, "in the future," when he came to the end of his rope, he came to himself, and he returned home.

Our duty as fathers is to remain faithful in the now. God's promise to us in the future, underscored in Deuteronomy 6:20, where the Scripture say, if we do our part, God will do His part, "in the future...." and bring our child back. Mighty Men remain faithful!

I know Christian parents who have had a child go out into the world, for a season, but eventually, that child came home. Their testimony to you is not to lose heart if your child hasn't yet returned. Stay faithful, keep praying, and keep watching.

Children have a role, too.

In Deuteronomy 6:20, Moses wrote that the day would come when our children will ask us, "What is the meaning of all of this...?" We can't make our children love Jesus. We can make sure they attend classes, and we can make them attend church. But there comes a time in their spiritual life that they have choices to make as well. Jesus will never forcefully enter a person's life. There are times when children, reared in the best of homes, go astray. When that happens, we need to take a good look at ourselves and be willing to make any necessary course corrections. But continuously beating ourselves up for our failures serves no useful purpose. "If we confess our sins, He is faithful and just to forgive our sins, and to cleanse us from all unrighteousness" (1 John1:9).

Jeremiah 29:11-12 is a great passage for you if you are a parent filled with guilt from failings in the past. It says, "For I know the plans I have for you, declares the Lord. Plans to prosper you and not to harm you, plans to give you hope and a future. Then you will call upon me, come and pray to me, and I will listen."

The greatest privilege

The greatest privilege of parenting is to pray for our children. Guess what Jesus is doing right now? He is praying for you and me. "He ever liveth to make intercession for us" (Hebrews 7:25). Of all the things the Lord Jesus could be doing, He has chosen the highest, and it is to sit down at the right hand of the Father and pray for us. You have been assigned the responsibility and privilege to be your child's Number One prayer intercessor. Who knows them better than you? Who loves them more than you do? Mighty Men pray for their children.

The Bible says that "if two of you shall agree on earth touching anything that you shall ask, it will be done" (Matthew 18:19). That doesn't mean we should get the preacher to pray with us, though that is quite alright. It means we should pray with our wives. The two of you have the same interests for your children. God intended for our homes to be like a small church, where two parents unite together in His name (Matthew 18:20). When a husband and wife get on their knees together to pray, there is incredible power for good, for we know that God promises to be right there with them. Mighty Men pray with their wives.

Fathers, the most important advice I can give you for your personal enrichment, as well as the welfare of your children, is to learn to pray daily with your wife. If you haven't done this in the past, you may feel self-conscious at first. You may get resistance from your wife initially, but the benefits to your relationship with her make all the difficulty's pale by comparison. My wife and I pray together every day, including by phone when I am traveling, and we both can testify of many miracles that we have witnessed in our family, and beyond, as a result of our prayer life together.

One of the main reasons marriages are failing, and a primary reason we are losing our children is that parents have failed to faithfully uphold their most important responsibility, which is to pray for their children.

I know that prayer for our children is important because Scripture reveals to us that one day Satan came walking into the presence of God and began making accusations about mankind, seeking to humiliate God, in essence, saying, "God, you're a failure." Then God said, "But have you considered my servant Job, he is not like any other on earth?" In Job 1:4 we find out why Job stood out from all others living in the land, "Early in the morning he would sacrifice a burnt offering for each of them, his children, thinking that perhaps my children have sinned and cursed God in their hearts. This was Job's regular custom." Every day he prayed for his kids. Do you do that?

God's part is "in the future...." Our part is now. When we pray in His will, God always hears and answers our prayers. It is God's will for our children to make it in this evil world. When did God ever need lights to shine more than now? When did God ever need a church to rise and be a church more than now? When did God ever need godly men more than now? Now is the time for Mighty Men to step up!

The greatest calling of parenting is to mentor our children. The highest responsibility of parenting is to pray for our children. And, the highest honor of parenting is modeling Christ.

Mighty Men model Christ

Here is how we can model Christ. Learn to deal properly with your successes and your failures. When you succeed, give all the glory to God, who both willed and accomplished His great pleasure through you. When you fail, own up to it and humble yourself. "If we confess our sins, He is faithful and just to forgive us our sins and to cleanse us from all unrighteousness" (1 John 1:9). When we blow it, we need to admit we failed and ask God's forgiveness. Then we need to approach those who saw us blow it and ask for their forgiveness. The bitterest child cannot ignore a parent who says, "I blew it and I'm so sorry. Please forgive me." They may not respond favorably right away, but they will never forget it. We need to deal with our failures. And remember that God's part is "in the future."

Remember that our Father in Heaven is merciful and tenderhearted. Therefore, we too should be merciful and tenderhearted. Ephesians 4:32 says, "Be kind and compassionate one to the other." That means husbands, wives and their children should be kind and tenderhearted towards each other. It goes on to say, "forgiving each other just as in Christ, God forgave you."

God intended for us to strive to live in such a way that someday when our children hear that God is known as their Father, they will have memories they cherish because their earthly father was faithful, caring, tender hearted, loving, and always compassionate, even when administering discipline. When I have failed in the past, I wanted to run to my caring God and find forgiveness and understanding. I have reared three teenagers, and all of them have failed at times along the way. Every one of them needed a father to whom they could run to and obtain forgiveness and understanding. Your children will come to you if you imitate God. They will run from you if you don't. Mighty Men are tenderhearted.

Just as the 100-meter sprint goes by in the blink of an eye, so do the years of child rearing. God has given us an excellent handbook to help us, but we must commit to spending time in it and time with its Author.

We must keep the things that God has taught us in our hearts. Fear God and obey Him. We should impress them on our children by talking about them "when we sit at home, when we walk along the road, when we lie down and when we get up." These truths should be reflected in our homes and even on our persons. Above all else, we must remember to "love the Lord our God with all our heart and with all our soul and with all our strength." Then, when the race is over and we're contemplating how quickly it passed by, we will be able to rest in the knowledge that we have won the victory in Christ. Mighty Men are like that.

Chapter Five

HOW TO MANAGE TEENAGERS

"The Hammer Throw"

The sport of hammer throwing dates back to ancient times, and it typically attracted athletes who were big, bulky, and vigorous. In some ways, rearing teenagers successfully is similar to competing in the hammer throw. I'm not suggesting that frustrated parents start throwing hammers!

Today, the reign of the giants is over, and athletes with sturdy physiques, perfect timing, and great technique, dominate the hammer throw. They have a full range of athletic abilities including speed, agility, strength, and suppleness. Success depends on the thrower's ability to overcome the effects of centrifugal force and the pull of the hammer while spinning at a great speed within a small, defined space.

The thrower stands in a circle seven feet in diameter. The hammer weighs 16 pounds, and consists of a heavy ball attached to a metal handle with a wire. The whole device is no longer than 4 feet. The athlete grips the handle of the hammer firmly and with his feet remaining stationary, begins to twirl the ball in a circle above and behind his head and below his knees. As the hammer gains momentum, the thrower whirls his body around three times to increase velocity before releasing the ball upward and outward at a 45-degree angle. If it falls outside a prescribed 90-degree arc, the throw is invalid. If the hammer or any part of the thrower's body touches the ground outside the circle before the release is complete, a foul is called.

High school athletes do not participate in this event because, like the javelin, it's too dangerous. This element of danger is where the sport begins to remind me of raising teenagers. It can be a precarious undertaking. After raising three of them, I can attest that I prepared and delivered my most evocative sermons on rearing teenagers— before I had one.

The importance of coaching

The first similarity between the hammer throw and raising teenagers is this: Like the throwers, teens need coaching. No hammer thrower does well on his own; at least not at first. Some possess raw, brute strength and a certain amount of athletic ability, and can accomplish more than others. But the reality is, hammer throwers, just like teens, need a lot of instruction.

Proverbs 22:6 says, "Train up a child in the way that he should go and when he is old he will not depart from it." This verse is a vital reminder to all of us that rearing teenagers requires time and commitment. The Hebrew word which we translate "train," presupposes that the parent will discern the bent of the child, that is, their natural propensities, and then guide them toward occupations that capitalize on their natural strengths and passions. In context, I believe that it means the father will encourage, but not force, the child to pursue that for which he is best suited and will provide the tools he needs to be successful. Tragically, many men are more apt to do that with sports than they are with the more important matters that might assist the child to be successful later in their careers.

So, how does a father do this? Successful coaches get to know their throwers well. They're around them constantly. For many hours of the day, they watch them, videotape them, and study their technique. A good coach, who wants to produce a champion, soon learns the strengths and the weaknesses of his athlete instinctively. They then work to perfect their athlete's strengths.

God never intended our teenagers to enter the world in the raw, without supervision. God gives every child natural gifts and talents. It's the father's duty to build on those strengths, just as a coach does with his athlete. Good parents make sacrifices of time and treasure so their child can best compete in the arena of life with their unique gifts. This sacrifice may involve making long trips across town for supplemental coaching, or investing in an instrument or expensive piece of equipment. Good parents invest in their children.

We also need to observe their weaknesses and address them. In the first chapter of James, a man is described who wakes up in the morning, peers into a mirror, and notices that his appearance is unkempt. But then he turns away and does nothing to address what he observed. He enters the world completely unprepared. Many of us not only do that in our personal lives, but also in the lives of our children.

A wise coach encourages his athlete to believe in himself and be the best he can be. The coaches I remember with the greatest affection from college and high school were the ones who reinforced me with encouragement and praise. My least pleasant memories are of coaches who chose humiliation and cursing to get their points across, like "Scarborough, you're the worst blocker on the team." Few athletes respond to negativism...and fewer teenagers! When it comes to parenting, the adage is spot on: "You raise what you praise." In fact, psychologists tell us that it takes as many as 13 positive comments from a parent to reinforce and overcome a single negative one. Children have a great need to be affirmed by their dads. And if they don't receive it at home, they'll look for it elsewhere. As fathers, we must remind ourselves of the importance of encouraging them to achieve their very best. Successful coaches know their thrower. Successful parents know their children. Mighty Men are encouragers.

You can't skip the fundamentals

Successful coaches teach the fundamentals to their athletes and teens need no less from their fathers. Tragically, most teenagers in our land are growing up with little or no training from dad's regarding God's infallible Word. As fathers who want to be Mighty Men, you have the responsibility to teach your teens the fundamentals of right and wrong.

This vital teaching begins in our homes, not in our church buildings. The church has our kids for just a small fraction of any given week. If we believe that a Sunday school teacher can do in 30 to 40 minutes, one day a week, what we are unwilling or unable to do in the multiple hours that we have with our teens, we are kidding ourselves. It is the father's responsibility to lay a Biblical foundational in the lives of their children.

There are three primary places where our teenagers can obtain truth and knowledge. The first is at home. The second is a sound local church were the Bible is proclaimed. The third is a good Christian school that comes alongside parents, reinforcing Biblical values and educational excellence.

This reinforcement in a good Christian school is of particular importance when you consider children often return home tired and worn out from a busy school day. And, the child is not the only one who's tired. Especially in a family where both parents are working outside the home. At this point, often the child is not in the best condition for receiving instruction, and the parent is not in the best shape to do any creative teaching.

For those who prefer to be their child's full-time teachers or cannot afford to send their child to a Christian school, homeschooling can be a great alternative. More and more parents across America are turning to homeschooling because it not only provides a one-on-one teaching environment, but saves money, allowing one parent to stay home during the day. Best of all, parents can be assured that their children are being taught Biblical values along with other curriculum.

I realize that homeschooling or private Christian education is not for every family. It's a decision that should be made with much prayerful and careful consideration. For those who have children in public schools, Christian teachers called to public education can provide an oasis in an otherwise antagonistic environment, encouraging Christian students to stay true to their faith. A wise father can discern which option is best for his children, but I encourage Christian education if possible.

I entreat anyone who must send children to public schools to do so with care. Regardless of which avenue you choose, you must devote time to your teen's welfare. It takes time to monitor a child's education and hold your children and their teachers accountable. People don't often do what you expect; but rather what you inspect. All of us have a sin nature that has to be consistently held accountable under the Lordship of Christ. You and I have a responsibility to be accountable to God and to one another. You must lay that foundation for your teenager, whether through Christian education, (either in a private school or homeschooling), or public education, and you must monitor the whole process.

Knowing when to seek help

Coaches often take an athlete to a certain point and then refer them to other coaches who can help them improve their abilities in a particular area. A good coach, like Clint Eastwood's character in *Dirty Harry*, "knows his limitations." Good fathers know their limitations too. You must learn to know when to supplement your teen's training.

And then finally, a good coach will model what he's teaching to his student athletes. I once had an English teacher who wrote across my paper a word I couldn't make out. I asked, "What does this say?" And the teacher looked at me and said, straight-faced, "Penmanship.

Son, your penmanship is awful." I've never forgotten the irony of a teacher, who couldn't write well, criticizing my penmanship. I did work on my handwriting after that, but I always responded better to people who modeled what they taught. And, so do teenagers.

If you are living and indulging in destructive behaviors, don't be surprised when your children do so as well. Though none of us is perfect, we all have to strive to model what we preach and teach. Mighty Men understand that.

Another trait of successful coaches is that they're honest. No one, especially a teenager, wants a parent looking them right in the eye and telling them things that just aren't true. I've heard men say things like, "Son, you're the best. You ought to be the quarterback. You're the best one out there," when everyone listening, including the son, knew he was not. Most teens are more self-aware than that. When the teenager knows full well that he's not the best quarterback, such rhetoric rings hollow. A great coach says to the athlete, "You know, son, you're not going to win the first team job, but through hard work, you can improve, and we need you be ready to step in and lead if our starter is hurt. You can be a lot better if you dedicate yourself and help this team." No one has much regard for dishonesty. Everyone thrives in an atmosphere of honesty. Your teen will appreciate your honesty to them. "You shall know the truth and the truth shall set you free" (John 8:32).

Successful coaches commit to their athletes unselfishly in both success and disappointment. One of the greatest illustrations of this in my memory occurred during the 1982 NCAA men's basketball final between the Georgetown Hoyas and the University of North Carolina Tar Heels. The Hoyas led late in the game, but a shot by Michael Jordan gave North Carolina the lead. Georgetown still had a chance to win in the final seconds, but Freddy Brown threw an infamous bad pass to opposing player James Worthy, sealing Georgetown's defeat.

Brown was understandably distraught, and sportscasters seized on the moment. They shoved a microphone into the face of Hall of Fame Coach John Thompson and said, "Isn't it a tragedy that your player blew it? In the big moment, he blew it."

The coach responded, "What do you mean he blew it? This kid got us here!" He then hugged Freddy Brown and told him he'd get another chance. The next year, Georgetown won the national championship. That's what a great coach does. He doesn't throw the kid under the bus because he made a mistake. And there's a lesson here for every dad rearing a teen. Mighty Men get that.

Living by the rules

Okay, we've established that, like hammer throwers and other athletes, teens need coaching. Another similarity is that they like to compete. However, before they can compete, they must learn the rules and be taught to value them. Living by the rules is not as easy as it sounds. We're residing in a violent culture that has lost the sense of the importance of standards. Fathers must teach their teenager that rules are in place, to help us, not hurt us. God's rule book, the Bible, has been preserved for our wellbeing.

Imagine a tiny Chihuahua dog, playing inside a chain link fence. Chihuahuas, some of which you can carry in your shirt pocket, are notorious for snarling and barking as if they intend to rip a bigger dog to shreds!

However, for all his seeming ferocity, a Chihuahua is quite grateful for a fence protecting him from the larger dog. Teenagers are a lot like that little Chihuahua. They may bark their demands for freedom, while secretly hoping you will restrain them.

What do you think would happen if the bigger dog suddenly got inside the fence with the Chihuahua? The yapping Chihuahua would race to the corner looking for a hiding place and hoping for an intervention. Our teenagers cannot thrive in a world without fences. God's Word provides protection from the outside world.

As a parent, I know that after listening to a teenager yap awhile, we're tempted to say, "Alright, Alright!! Go. I don't care. Get out of here." But Mighty Men know better. Teenagers want someone who cares enough to restrain them. Through the experience of rearing teenagers into adults, and by much observation over the years, I've found that when it comes to more freedom, teens seldom think there is ever enough. When you depart from God's standards to "preserve the peace" with a teen, they soon demand more and more ground. Be forewarned—appeasement never works. It results in tragedy.

A Lesson from History

British Prime Minister Neville Chamberlain realized, too late, that appeasement was not the answer when Adolf Hitler began marching through Europe, grabbing up land and wreaking havoc. After signing the Munich pact in September 1938, he came back to London proclaiming that he had brought peace with honor. He said, "I believe it is peace for our time. We thank you from the bottom of our hearts. Go home and get a nice, quiet sleep." But Europe soon discovered what God's Word underscores: There can be no peace with evil. Hitler swept his armies into Poland, igniting World War II.

Successful coaches will teach their athletes to value the rules. Without them, there can be no competition. Without rules, there can't be a declared winner. Without rules, as the English philosopher Thomas Hobbes put it, life would be "solitary, poor, nasty, brutish and short." The Bible tells us that God put a hedge around us, not to confine us, but to protect us from the evil beyond. In the book of Proverbs 28:13 we are reminded that without God's vision for righteousness, people throw off off restraints. Hammer throwers, like teenagers, need to compete, to learn the rules and to value the rules.

Right Choices Must be Made

Champions must make choices daily with the future in view if they're going to compete successfully. They must avoid destructive behavior, and sacrifice immediate gratification for future rewards.

In fact, that's true for everyone who wants to accomplish something of merit in life.

Athletes don't get to the Olympics by going to parties. They live in the quieter realm of self-discipline, anticipating a future reward. As fathers, we must inculcate our teens with the reality that everything they do today has a direct correlation with tomorrow. We must communicate to our teenagers that they don't just live in the present. Also—and every parent knows what I'm talking about here—we must impress upon them that they are not invincible. Scripture tells us that Satan, like a prowling lion, is seeking whom he may devour and your precious teen is his prey, if left unprotected. It is the coach's responsibility to warn the athlete, and it's the father's responsibility to advise the teenager.

Overcoming Inertia

Teenagers are also similar to hammer throwers in that they have to master certain life skills. First, they must overcome inertia. Getting moving is not easy with the hammer throw or a teenager. Regarding the hammer, that heavy metal ball doesn't want to move. You have to overcome inertia to move it. Launching our teens in the right direction is likewise difficult, but it is the responsibility of fathers to see that it happens. You must get them moving and give them proper guidance. With God's help you can enable them to see the need to overcome spiritual inertia.

Stay Within the Boundaries

Secondly, they must learn to stay within boundaries. It's our job, once the lines are clearly established and communicated, to make sure they stay within the boundaries. As the teen grows older and matures, those boundaries change. If we were to put a professional athlete in a Little League ballpark, he'd be frustrated. There'd be no challenge or any motivation to excel. Teenagers are the same way about rules.

Wise coaches recognize when a student is ready to move on to the next challenge. And wise fathers understand when boundaries must be relaxed. Unless the boundaries match the maturity level of the teenager, we will destroy them or at least damage their prospects for a good life.

Know When to Release

Here's one more similarity between the hammer throw and rearing teenagers. As the thrower twirls the hammer faster and faster, it becomes more and more difficult for the thrower to stay balanced due to the increasing centrifugal force being generated. The faster he turns it, the more he must lean back to counterbalance the pull of the weight on the end of the wire.

For your teenager, the centrifugal force or, as we more commonly call it, the pull of the world is always increasing. It is unrelenting. It never stops. As their coach, if you allow them to relax, it will pull them outside the safe circle. The threat of injury or loss is constant.

In the hammer throw, the thrower endures an incredible pull on his back muscles. He's in constant danger of ripping a muscle completely in half and being permanently disabled. The hammer throw is a dangerous sport. Throwing the hammer in the wrong direction can damage others. Teenagers are like that. The danger of failure is ever present, it's ominous, and it can adversely affect others. Using their cell phone while driving, is but one illustration of many temptations your teen faces daily. They need a Mighty Man to survive.

The hammer thrower has to have incredible coordination and a near perfect sense of timing. Once he gets that weighty ball circling his head and gets his body moving, there so much complete energy being generated that he must summon all of his training to know when to let go. The hammer has to hit within defined lines. If it hits too far to the right or left, the throw is disqualified. Very few hammer throwers can hit the middle, straight line, dead-on and no one can do it twice.

When rearing teenagers, we have to know how much to pull back and when to let go. It can be dizzying. In fact, everybody in the circle can be pulled off balance if we're not careful. If we let go too soon, the teen will land out of bounds to the right. If we let go too late, they'll hit to the left. Mighty Men realize early on how important it is to pray and depend on God for a good outcome.

If it seems there aren't many perfect kids out there, it's because imperfect parents are rearing them and the centrifugal forces are too great. The challenge for all dads is to, know just how fast to spin your teenager without losing your balance and, remain aware of when to release them to give them the best chance of success.

An Example of a Perfect Father

Often, we won't find out how well we did until years later. The greatest analogy of a successful hammer thrower in the Bible is contained in the story of the Prodigal Son. The son came to his father's house one day and said, "I want out of here. I want what's mine. Give it to me." Essentially, what this brash and ungrateful son said was, "I wish you were dead. Give me my inheritance."

Teenagers can be like that. They can be very cruel at times. That's part of the centrifugal force. To overcome it, a father must learn how to love the unlovable, restrain the unrestrainable, and even forgive the almost unforgivable. Teenagers are not always unlovable but sometimes they can provoke a parent to utter harsh words resulting in a schism that will seem beyond repair. But explosions can be avoided if the parent is Spirit-controlled. Fathers of teenagers need to learn to resist letting hotheaded tension pull them off balance.

The key is to depend on God. By turning to Him, we can learn to love the unlovable. Christ will show us how to restrain our kids. Teens will act as though they don't want to be monitored, yet we need to do so for their good. In the story of the Prodigal Son, when the son demanded, "I can go do my own thing. Give me mine," the father did. The most remarkable part of the Scripture to me as a father is that when the child blew it all and wound up in the pigpen, his father didn't go after him. What he did do, was pray. He recognized that if God's Spirit did not find the child and turn the child's heart back toward home, all the money in the world would not rescue him. Any fix he could offer would ultimately be temporary and result in more harm down the road. Though we might be able to modify outer behavior, sin is a problem of the heart. You may have a broken heart because of a wayward child right now, but as much as you may want to, bringing them home before they are ready, is the worst thing you can do for your child.

The Father of the Prodigal Son never gave up hope. The reason he saw that boy returning home, before anyone else, was that he was the only one looking for him. The Bible doesn't say what the father did while he was waiting, but I suspect that he spent much of his time in prayer. I imagine that when he finished his prayer time each day, he looked down the lane to see if his beloved son was coming home. And every day when there was no son in sight, he'd just go back to the prayer closet and pray some more, because that father knew that God was watching over his son. In a sense, he was merely a franchise holder. His Father in Heaven owned the son and understood his wayward behavior. His Father in Heaven knew where he was, and cared deeply about the son.

That Dad went to God and said, "Lord, help me." And the Holy Spirit went to the son, mired in the slop of the pigpen, and began working on his conscience, reminding him how much his father loved him. The Bible says that the son finally came to himself and said, "Look at me. Look where I'm living and look how I'm living. In my father's house, the servants have it better." And so, he headed home in tattered clothes without a ring on his finger or shoes on his feet. He was determined to beg his father to let him be one of the servants. He had scripted it all out in his mind. "When I see my dad, I'm going to say, 'Father, I have sinned against heaven and before you, and I am no longer worthy to be your son. Make me a hired servant.'" He was so distant from his father that he feared there was no love left. However, when his father saw him coming, the father ran to him, threw his arms around him and hugged him.

The father then let him give his speech until the final phrase. The Son said, "Father, I have sinned against heaven and in your sight, and I am no more worthy to be your son." But before he could say "make me a servant," the father reclaimed him as a son. He put a brand new robe on his shoulders, shoes on his feet, and a ring on his finger, signifying his sonship. He ignored the stench and the filth of the pig pen and chose not to remind him of his failure. Rather, he celebrated his future and threw him a party.

I want to say to every father with a wayward child that God still operates if we will cooperate. Nothing has changed. His arms are not so short that he cannot reach down to the pig sty where a child may be. Success in rearing teenagers will hinge on our being good coaches, equipping them to compete and master the life skills necessary to land within the boundaries. And remember, during those tuff times that rob you of your rest, worrying, you have a Head Coach in Heaven who is watching over you and your teenager is as well. Mighty Men get that!

Chapter Six

HOW TO CONTROL YOUR TONGUE

"The Javelin Throw"

One event in track and field that I have never attempted is the javelin throw. When I was in high school, the event wasn't allowed because it was so dangerous. I knew very little about the event. However, I do remember that my old high school coach would occasionally comment, "Scarborough if you were on the track team and we threw the javelin, I'd let you catch it." I don't think that was a compliment.

The javelin is a long spear-like instrument made up of three parts: the shaft, head, and grip. With its pointed head, the javelin is designed to be flung through the air. Some athletes can throw it more than 300 feet. Jan Zelezny of Czechoslovakia holds the current world record, which he set on May 25, 1996, with a stunning throw of 323 feet, 1 inch. A football field is 300 feet long, which will help you appreciate just how far Jan Zelezny hoisted his record throw.

In the javelin throw, you get three opportunities to establish your mark. The top seven throwers move on to the finals, and each receives three more throws. To be counted as a throw, the javelin has to be planted in the turf and stand. If it bounces, the throw is disqualified. This event requires an enormous amount of skill, strength, and coordination. The competitor must throw the javelin on a straight line, landing within an eight-foot wide channel.

In times past, a man used the javelin to kill game and feed his family. It was also used as a weapon, so it has real potential for good and harm.

The javelin is a lot like the spear in our mouths—the human tongue, which, likewise, has enormous potential for good and for harm. It is a 2 ounce, 4-inch long mucous membrane, wrapped around an assortment of nerves and muscles, designed to help us to eat and talk. That sounds innocent enough, but the truth is, we often eat and say too much!

Nothing in the world has greater capacity for good or for evil. The Greek philosopher Publius said, "I have often regretted my speech but never my silence." While I wouldn't go quite that far, I would agree that I have seldom regretted my silence, while often regretting my speech. Proverbs 10:19 says, "When words are many, sin is unavoidable. He who holds his tongue is wise."

In 1993, Dr. James Dobson wrote in his book, *Love for a Life-time*, that women speak 50,000 words per day, while men speak only 25,000. In the same year, marriage counselor Gary Smalley wrote a small pamphlet entitled *Connecting with Your Husband*, in which he said the average male uses about 12,000 words per day while a woman averages 25,000 words.

I'm not sure who's right, but one thing is certain—women are much more conversational and relational than men. It's logical to assume that they speak more words than men do. One author put the situation this way when he said, "My dilemma is this: When I arrive home, at five or six in the evening, I have already used my 25,000 words, and she hasn't even started yet."

I'm sure countless husbands and wives feel like that may be their problem. When two women go out to lunch, they talk from the time they meet until they leave each other's company. Put two men in a boat for half a day of fishing, and the conversation goes something like this: "Get any bites?" Answer: "Nope." When their wives want to know what they talked about, the men shrug and look at them.

I often hear women say, "He just won't talk." In fact, I have often heard my wife say that about me. The truth is that my best conversation time is when I can't sleep, and she's about to drop into Neverland. I usually want to talk after she's already asleep.

The tongue can be joyful and encouraging

Let's first examine the incredible potential of our tongues to be used for good. "Do not let any unwholesome talk come out of your mouths, but only that which is helpful for building others up according to their needs, that it may benefit those who listen" (Ephesians 4:29).

John Maxwell, a popular Christian author, wrote a book entitled *Developing the Leader Within You*. He suggests something very wise: "During the first 60 seconds of every new conversation, we should say something positive." Scripture says that we are to "encourage each other while it's still called today" (Hebrews 10:13). Simply put, offering encouragement should become second nature.

Think about those occasions when you're headed home after a busy day. If you're married, the wife and children are looking forward to seeing you, especially if the children are small. Teenagers typically don't sit at the curtains waiting for Daddy to come home, but those little ones do.

You pull around the corner and approach home, so excited to see your children. But as you prepare to turn into the driveway, you notice Johnny's bicycle blocking the way. You forget the little guy has looked forward to your arrival all day. Instead, you're thinking about "the rule," that says the bike is to be put up every evening. Now, rather than a wonderful time with your family, all you can think about is the broken rule. To add insult to injury, a passerby honks because you're blocking the roadway.

As you put away the bicycle, frustration builds. You walk into the house after thinking all the way home about a pleasant time with your family, and instead, you bark at little Johnny about his disobedience. The tone is set for the rest of the evening.

How different it could be if we could discipline ourselves to remember to be joyful and encouraging during the first 60 seconds we're home. Mighty Men do! There will be plenty of time later to address the matter of the bicycle, and by then you will have cooled down enough to address it civilly. The Bible says, "Do not let any unwholesome talk come out of your mouths, but only what is helpful for building others up according to their needs, that it may benefit those who listen." (Ephesians 4:29). What a difference it would make in our homes if we decided to practice the 60-second principle in every conversation.

The tongue can edify

Edify means to build up. It is similar to the word encourage, but is more foundational in meaning. Encouraging speech shores up; edifying speech builds up. Ephesians 4:29 is very appropriate, but so is Ephesians 5:19, where Paul writes, "speak to one another with psalms, hymns, and spiritual songs. Sing and make music in your heart to the Lord." Paul was addressing the manner in which Mighty Men speak to their wives. I wonder what would happen in our homes if we learned to practice meditating on God's Word and singing praise choruses in our hearts. "Out of the overflow of the heart, the mouth speaks" (Matthew 12:34). What kind of an atmosphere would we create if our seasoned responses reflected a heart focused on bringing glory to God? Our tongue has incredible potential for creating a healthy, happy environment, building up those who live in our presence, if we're intentional about doing so. Mighty Men do!

The tongue can defend

Here is where I cannot fully agree with the Greek philosopher Publius, whom I mentioned earlier. He said his silence had never embarrassed him. Really? It has me. There have been times when I should have spoken on behalf of the defenseless, and I didn't. The Bible says that we have in our mouths a tool that can help those who cannot help themselves. Proverbs 31:8-9 commands us to… "Speak up for those who cannot help themselves, for the rights of all who are destitute. Speak up and judge fairly, defend the rights of the poor and needy." Mighty Men do that! What about the rights and needs of the unborn who are routinely dismembered in our calloused society in the name of a woman's "right to choose?" Are we speaking up for them? And what about Christians who are being beheaded and burned alive for their faith all over the Middle East and parts of Africa? The silence of the church is deafening. Shame on us!

The tongue can praise

There is no higher purpose for our tongue than praise. In Proverbs 31:28, wise Solomon writes, "Her children arise and call her blessed; her husband also, and he praises her." Men, have you considered that God placed within your anatomy an instrument of praise that has the potential for exalting God and lifting the hearts of others?

Regarding our children, someone has said that you "raise what you praise." I'm often amazed at things I hear some men say to their children. They wound their own children with words that they would never utter to a neighbor's child, or a stranger, under any circumstances.

God gave you a tongue for praise. May we be like the Psalmist who wrote: "I will exalt you, my God the King; I will praise your name for ever and ever. Every day I will praise you and extol your name for ever and ever. Great is the Lord and most worthy of praise; his greatness no one can fathom. One generation commends your works to another; they tell of your mighty acts. They speak of the glorious splendor of your majesty—and I will meditate on your wonderful works. (Psalm 145:1-6) The tongue can praise. Mighty Men do!

The tongue can heal

Solomon wisely said, "Reckless words pierce like a sword but the tongue of the wise (Mighty Men) brings healing" (Proverbs 12:18). During those years of watching our children play various sports, I would occasionally see a coach unintentionally inflict great pain on a child. We all should coach a Little League team at least once. The experience would make us more sympathetic toward volunteer coaches. But we should never lightly dismiss those times when reckless words pierce a child. Trying to manage 20 to 30 kids and, at the same time, keep up with all of the activities going on around them, it's easy for a coach to damage a child with a careless word: "Good grief, don't just stand there, Johnny—Swing!" Or... "Catch the ball for once!"

On more than one occasion I witnessed one of our children's countenance fall due to a coach's comment. Nothing could heal their hurts as quickly as my being there to put my arm around them and offer words of encouragement. I'd like to say I was always that sensitive, but I wasn't. Offering healing words requires work and prayer for most men. Those who are willing to invest the time and prayer into becoming sensitive to others will become Mighty Men. The good news is that God promises that, "We can be confident of this: He Who began a good work in you will be faithful to complete it" (Philippians 1:6). It might not be easy, but it is certainly attainable and worth every effort!

We have within us an instrument that God has designed to bring healing. We must remember as we move about in this hurting world that we are passing multitudes of people smiling on the outside but dying on the inside every day. Saying just the right word can promote healing if we're discerning and available. Isaiah the prophet says, "The Sovereign Lord has given me a well-instructed tongue, that I may know the word to sustain the weary. He awakens my ear to listen, to listen as one being taught" (Isaiah 50:26). Every day we should ask God to speak through us—to give us the word that He alone knows someone needs to hear. A hurting teenager or a hurting friend might be right next to us. If we are sensitive to our surroundings, we will meet hurting, broken people every day. We have the power within our mouths to mend their broken hearts. Sometimes, a simple phone call can communicate the words that lift someone out of their pit of despair. Your tongue has the potential to bring healing. Mighty Men do that!

The tongue can teach

"The tongue of the wise (Mighty Men) commends knowledge" (Proverbs 15:2). You have spent your entire life to date accumulating knowledge and understanding. You can instruct others who have less experience in life. We can use our tongues to commend knowledge and help others avoid the pitfalls we've encountered. Everyone reading this book has the capacity, and more importantly, the responsibility, to impart the knowledge that God has given them. Mighty Men do!

The tongue can express gratitude

The Bible says, "In everything give thanks for this is the will of God in Christ Jesus concerning you" (1 Thessalonians 5:18). A thankful heart is the most valuable gift we can offer our gracious God. How often do you remember to thank God for the marvelous things He has done in your life? It must ache His heart when we fail to say, "thank you, Father." Paul also said that "Godliness with contentment is great gain" (1 Timothy 6:6). Contentment promotes gratitude. A contented person isn't always striving for more, but instead, has an appreciation for what God has already provided in their life.

Many of us spend too much time complaining, and too little showing gratitude. You may have a problem that seems overwhelming, but consider this: God could have prevented it had He chosen.

Scripture says, "When times are good, be happy, but when times are bad, consider that God has made the one as well as the other" (Ecclesiastes 7:14). Since we know that God loves us and wants us to succeed in life, we can conclude that no matter how bad something is at present, he has a purpose for allowing it and a plan for working it out for our best. The Scripture says, "And we know that all things work together for good to them that love God, to them who are the called according to his purpose" (Romans 8:28 KJV). Scripture also states, "My thoughts toward you are good and not evil all the days of your life" (Jeremiah 29:11). If those verses are true, and we know they are, then it follows that even in the worst circumstance, we can, by faith, thank Him. We are not thankful for the terrible thing which may be happening to us, but while the terrible thing is happening, we can believe, by faith, that He knows what He is doing. He promises us that "When (not if!) you walk through the water, the waves will not sweep over you. When you walk through the fire, you will not be burned. For I am the Lord your God … Do not fear, for I am with you" (Isaiah 43:2, 5).

When we release our faith, we can rest assured that in His time, not ours, He will do something supernatural, and we will see that the Scriptures are true. The writer of Hebrews says that "Without faith, it is impossible to please God" (Hebrews 11:6a). Consider Joseph. Rising above his darkest days, Joseph said to his brothers, who sold him into slavery: "But as for you, you meant evil against me; but God meant it for good…" (Genesis 50:20). God turned the evil that was intended for Joseph into His provision, and Joseph testified of it for the rest of his days as evidence of God's love and mercy. In fact, we're still talking about it now!

Moses' life is another great example of this spiritual truth. He was banished from Egypt to the backside of the desert for the next 40 years because he struck down an Egyptian, thinking he was doing God's will. He could have lived in abject bitterness, complaining, "God, I did my best and here's where it got me." Instead, out of those 40 years of brokenness, God developed a Mighty Man of God. He brought him back to be one of the greatest leaders the world has ever known.

I don't want to trivialize anyone's suffering. My wife has a cousin, a few years older than she, who was stricken with polio when she was 13. She has lived her entire life in her home, near the iron lung that has enabled her to breathe and live. I don't know why God allowed that to happen. I don't know why our youngest daughter, to whom I have dedicated this book, was called to her reward at the young age of 25, but I know that God has a plan, and at least part of that plan is for me to trust Him and live in His love. I choose to praise Him in all things, even when I don't understand it. And I have made an incredible discovery in life: Faith works and in time, becomes sight.

The tongue has the potential to give thanks. Mighty Men do that!

The tongue can pray

James says in his epistle: "Is anyone among you in trouble? Let them pray. Is anyone happy? Let them sing songs of praise. Is anyone among you sick? Let them call the elders of the church to pray over them and anoint them with oil in the name of the Lord. And the prayer offered in faith will make the sick person well; the Lord will raise them up. If they have sinned, they will be forgiven" (James 5:13-15).

Do you realize that you and I can bow our heads in faith and shape the course of mankind and nations through prayer? Do you realize that within us is the capacity to shape world events and influence world leaders? Do you realize that God has given us access to the King of Kings and Lord of Lords? Hebrews 14:6 tells us to "Approach God's throne of grace with confidence so that we may receive mercy and find grace to help in our time of need." When you come in Jesus' name with a pure heart and clean hands, He listens, and He responds. "The faithful, fervent prayer of a righteous man is powerful and effective" (James 5:16).

Volumes have been written on this subject. I feel guilty just penning a few paragraphs about prayer, for it is in many ways the essence of the Christian life. But the purpose of this chapter is to remind men of several wonderful things the tongue can do—none of which can surpass the potential found in a prayer. Just consider one mighty truth, "Jesus ever liveth to make intercession for us" (Hebrews 7:25). If prayer is that important to Him, it should be important to those who follow Him. Mighty Men pray!

The tongue can preach

God did not call everyone to be a pastor, but every one of us can preach. Preaching is sharing the story of God's infinite love. We have all been called to convey His love to a hurting and desperate world. Our lives are our message. What are we preaching to those with whom we live, work and socialize?

Through all the ages, many have tried to find a better way to share the Gospel than through preaching. Some churches now advertise that they don't have preaching; they just sing and share testimonies. That certainly has its important place, but God has chosen to transform lives by the "foolishness" of preaching.

Paul wrote in 1 Corinthians 1:19; "For the preaching of the cross is foolishness to them that perish; but unto us which are saved it is the power of God." Notice, it says "foolishness." This world will always think it's foolish, but it is the power of God to salvation (see Romans 1:16).

Preaching has greatly influenced my life. Many of us came to Christ because somebody stammered and stuttered and preached in the power of God. Look at the effect it has had on our nation. In his epic work, *Democracy in America,* completed in 1840, Alexis de Tocqueville credited the pulpits of America for the greatness of the nation. Do you realize that you have in your mouth an instrument capable of sharing the life-giving words of Jesus? God can use you to preach. Mighty Men do—not as a profession, but as a lifestyle!

Finally, let's look at the tenth potential for good.

The tongue can call

In Romans 10:13, Paul writes: "Everyone who calls on the name of the Lord will be saved." Salvation comes when someone calls on the name of Jesus. No number of good deeds that we do for others can bring us salvation. There is nothing we can do to earn it. Salvation is a free gift—we simply have to call on His name, in faith, to receive it. Our tongue has the power to bring change to our lives for eternity, when we call upon Jesus. In fact, if you don't have the assurance of your salvation, you can settle that issue right now by praying the following prayer:

"Dear Jesus, I come before you because I have no assurance that if I were to die at this moment, I would go to heaven to be with you for eternity. I want to make things right with you today. I know in my heart that I am a sinner. Please forgive me for all the wrong I have done. I thank You for giving Your Son, Jesus, to die on the cross in payment for my sin. Therefore, I turn from my sin and place my trust in you. I accept that it is only by His blood that I can be washed clean before you. Wash me clean, dear Lord, and come into my heart and become Lord of my life. In Jesus' Name, I pray, Amen."

The tongue has potential for harm

The tongue has enormous potential for good. But while the tongue can do incredible good, it also has incredible potential for harm. James 3:6 says, "The tongue also is a fire, a world of evil … it corrupts the whole person." Let's examine eight of the ways a tongue can bring harm.

The tongue can criticize

As I wrote earlier, Ephesians 4:29 says, "Do not let any unwholesome talk come out of your mouths, but only what is helpful for building others up, that it may benefit those who listen." Many of us fall victim to the temptation to criticize others. Nothing could be further from edification than criticism. One builds up, the other tears down. It's easy to look across the hall at work, or across the room at home, or from a pew across a church and criticize others. And, though there is a discipline known as constructive criticism, destructive criticism is more often the choice.

Criticism often stirs up strife. Scripture states that the Lord hates the man who stirs up dissension (see Proverbs 6:19). In Proverbs 11:12 Solomon instructs: "A man who lacks judgment derides his neighbor, but a man of understanding holds his tongue." Unwise criticism is as far from edification as the day is from night. God has given us an instrument in our mouths that, with God's help, can aid someone to become all that God desires. Not only does our criticism damage the one we criticize, it hurts others who are infected with our critical spirit. Lashing out with our tongue leaves everyone worse off rather than better. Mighty Men pray for others and avoid criticism!

The tongue can speak profanity

Proverbs 4:24 says, "Put away perversity from your mouth; keep corrupt talk far from your lips." We are living in an increasingly vulgar world where profanity is commonplace. Even the most educated people think nothing of using profane and unwholesome language, and previous generations seldom heard profanity spew forth from women. Today women are as likely to be profane as men.

James says, "With the tongue we curse men who have been made in God's likeness. Out of the same mouth come praise and cursing" (James 3:9). Webster defines cursing this way: "to blaspheme; to call upon the divine or supernatural power to send injury upon; to denounce in fervent and profane terms." James goes on to write in 3:10b-12, "My brothers this should not be. Can both fresh water and salt water flow from the same spring? Can a fig tree bear olives or a grapevine bear figs? Neither can a salt water spring produce fresh water." James presents the truth, that what comes out of our mouths is what's in our hearts. From the depths of the salt spring comes salt water. From an olive tree, we get olives. Our words reflect what is in our hearts. The key to bringing the tongue under control is yielding the heart to Christ.

Mighty Men present their tongues to Jesus and repent for speech that is profane. Profanity is speech that is impure, defiled, serving to debase or defile what is holy. In our culture today, swearing is relative, and the Bible is no longer the standard by which it is measured. Many have become so profane for so long that there is no longer a check in their spirits to tell them when something is impure. If you're one of those men, why not ask God now to help you modify your speech?

When I was in college, before I got serious about serving the Lord, I was very profane. I played football, and cursing was the norm for players. Then Jesus completely changed my life during the summer between my freshman and sophomore football seasons. I became super sensitive to my illicit speech, and was mortified that I might curse while around Christians, particularly in the church I started attending.

My filthy language became a major focus of my prayer life. Clearly, such praying pleases our Heavenly Father! Some time later, I realized I no longer cursed. I do not know when I stopped, but I do know that God delivered my speech. If you have a problem with cursing, He will deliver yours too, if you ask. Mighty Men don't curse or use profanity!

The tongue can spew poison

James 3:8 says: "But the tongue can no man tame; it is an unruly evil, full of deadly poison." Poison is a substance that can kill, injure, impair, or inhibit an individual in some capacity. Has your tongue ever had that effect on someone you know, perhaps someone you love?

Far too often, in the heat of anger, the words fly and we can injure someone so deeply that the offended person will always feel the pain. Sometimes a relationship is severed forever because we said something we should not have and have either hurt someone emotionally, or severely damaged their reputation.

There is an adage I was taught at a very young age, and at one time believed. "Sticks and stones may break my bones but words will never harm me." There are few lies bigger than that one. I remember many times when I have suffered severe physical and emotional pain. I've had both knees operated on after athletic injuries. I've had serious illnesses. I've had a fall while riding my horse, that required hospitalization, which left me recovering with a walker for quite some time. I've been in a car accident that severely injured two other people, who required extended hospital stays. I have experienced some things that really hurt, including burying a child. So have many people.

But without question, some of the greatest pains I have known in my life came by way of the tongue, and often the tongues of people who said they loved me. Words do hurt. Please don't tell your children that words don't hurt, because some of the deepest wounds they will bear will be from words they will hear being thrown around, often in their own household. The tongue can spew poison. Mighty Men guard against such speech.

The tongue can deceive

The Bible says in Proverbs 24:28 (KJV), "Do not...use your lips to deceive." It is rare that deception is viewed as sin in our society. In fact, we often hear the sentiment that if it hurts no one, it's okay. This attitude is akin to saying the ends justify the means. We see people of power in various levels of government deceiving the voters who placed them there. We see university professors misleading students with philosophies that say truth is relative. We find men and women behind pulpits disregarding God's Word and teaching their own thoughts as though they were Biblical truths.

The Bible has much to say about a person who uses his tongue to deceive. "A false witness will perish, and whoever listens to him will be destroyed forever" (Proverbs 21:28). "A false witness will not go unpunished, and he who pours out lies will perish" (Proverbs 19:9).

God takes His warnings concerning deceit a step further. He not only holds us accountable for what our tongue says, but for being in partnership with others who deceive. We read in Ephesians 5:6 & 7, "Let no man deceive you with empty words…God's wrath comes on those who are disobedient…do not be partners with them." We must discern deception, and remove ourselves from it. If we seek God's wisdom, He will give it, and through the power of the Holy Spirit, we will be able to discern empty or deceitful words. Why should we not partner with those who speak deception? As the verse says, it's because God's wrath comes on those who are disobedient.

Jesus tells us in John 8:44, "The devil was a murderer from the beginning, not holding to the truth, for there is no truth in him. When he lies, he speaks his native tongue, for he is a liar and the father of lies." When we use our tongues to deceive, we are speaking the enemy's language. That should be motive enough for avoiding deceptive speech.

God's Word is clear. The consequences are clear. Have you used the javelin in your mouth to deceive someone this week? I urge you to seek God's forgiveness and own up to the deception. Mighty Men value truth.

The tongue can gossip

In Romans 1:28-32, Paul writes about the decline of a society where sexual sin, including homosexuality, is winked at and accepted. He describes that generation as being the generation of gossip. Paul reveals the sinful nature and lawlessness of mankind, stating how God pours out His wrath on those who reject His laws. Because they turn away from God's instruction and guidance, He gives them over to a depraved mind.

The list of sins includes murderers, deceivers, gossipers, and slanderers. Read what Paul said:

> "Furthermore, just as they did not think it worthwhile to retain the knowledge of God, so God gave them over to a depraved mind, so that they do what ought not to be done. They have become filled with every kind of wickedness, evil, greed and depravity. They are full of envy, murder, strife, deceit and malice. They are gossipers, slanderers, God-haters, insolent, arrogant and boastful; they invent ways of doing evil; they disobey their parents; they have no understanding, no fidelity, no love, no mercy. Although they know God's righteous decree that those who do such things deserve death, they not only continue to do these very things but also approve of those who practice them."

This passage clearly demonstrates how serious the sin of gossip is to God. Solomon reminds us that "a perverse man stirs up dissension, and a gossip separates close friends" (Proverbs 16:28).

Have you attempted to defend participation in gossip by saying, "Well, it was just truth!" When "truth" is shared with someone who is neither part of the problem, nor the solution, it is gossip. Christians must accept how damaging gossip really is and repent of it. When we hear gossip, we have an opportunity to stop it with a simple question. Ask: "Have you taken that to the person of whom you're speaking?" So much gossip is nothing more than hearsay and exaggeration. The tragedy is that when it finally reaches a source that can correct it, it's to late.

Gossip is like emptying a feather pillow out of a window on the 19th floor of a high rise. By the time the feathers settle to the ground, they can never be collected again because the wind scatters them. Gossip, like a raging fire, quickly gets out of control. Mighty Men don't participate in gossip.

The tongue can slander

In Romans 1:28-31, we read that, because mankind did not think it worthwhile to retain the knowledge of God, He gave them over to a depraved mind, to do what they should not do. It says that every kind of wickedness and evil follows such behavior. Slander is listed right up there with murder. Most people agree that it's wrong to steal, and yet think nothing of taking someone's good name by slander. Proverbs 10:18 states, "Whoever spreads slander is a fool." And Proverbs 11:9 warns, "With his mouth, the godless destroys his neighbor."

We should not only refuse to spread slander or listen to it, but stop it when we hear it. If we don't attempt to stop it when it's spoken in our presence, we're just as guilty as though we spoke it ourselves. Slander dishonors God. Be assured that He will hold us accountable if we participate in such behavior. Mighty Men don't!

The tongue can kill

The Bible says, "The words of the wicked lie in wait for blood" (Proverbs 12:6) and, "The tongue has the power of life and death" (Proverbs 18:21). Depending on how it is used, your tongue can build up or tear down. It can kill trust, kill a testimony, kill a marriage, kill the sensitive spirit of a child, and kill a church. The tongue is powerful. The tongue is dangerous. The tongue is uncontrollable apart from God's divine intervention.

Let us also consider how God used words. God saw the world that was not, and He spoke, and the world came to be. Genesis 3 repeats over and over: "And God said…"

The Apostle John said, "In the beginning was the Word, and the Word was with God, and the Word *was* God. He was with God in the beginning. Through him all things were made; without Him, nothing was made that has been made … *the Word became flesh* and made His dwelling among us" (John 1:3-4, 14).

123

Jesus is the spoken Word ... made flesh. During His ministry on earth, He walked out and looked at a raging sea and spoke, and immediately it became calm (see Mark 4:35-41). Jesus could look at a dead man and say "arise" and he would come alive (see John 4:43). Jesus, who resides in believers, has bequeathed power to us, in His name, to do amazing things. It is an awesome power. But when power is not controlled and yielded to Christ, it becomes the power to destroy.

Because words have so much power to destroy, God gives a wonderful promise to those who walk with Him. "No weapon forged against you will prevail, and you will refute every tongue that accuses you. This is the heritage of the servants of the Lord, and this is their vindication from Me, declares the Lord" (Isaiah 54:17). What the enemy means for evil, God can use for good (Genesis 50:20).

We live in a world where men have learned how to tame giant whales, like Shamu. We can tame lions. I once saw a donkey jump off a 20-foot platform, into a pool of water, at the command of his master, yet we cannot tame the tongue. We live in a world that is torn apart because of the looseness of so many tongues.

God's plan for your tongue is for you to partner with Him to accomplish His purposes on this earth. "Call unto me and I will answer you and show you great and mighty things that you do not know" (Jeremiah 33:3). Though no one can tame the tongue, we can make it more and more like the tongue Jesus possessed. Just like a fire, the tongue has great potential for good and bad. That same fire, that warms on a cold winter's day, can set a whole house ablaze if it is not controlled. You can realize the highest good from your tongue when you are surrendered to the Lordship of Christ.

In Revelation 12, the Bible talks about the last great war between Satan and God.

"And there was war in heaven: Michael and his angels fought against the dragon; and the dragon fought and his angels, and prevailed not; neither was their place found any more in heaven. And the great dragon was cast out, that old serpent, called the Devil, and Satan, which deceiveth the whole world: he was cast out into the earth, and his angels were cast out with him. And I heard a loud voice saying in heaven, 'Now is come salvation, and strength, and the kingdom of our God, and the power of his Christ: for the accuser of our brethren is cast down, which accused them before our God day and night.' And they overcame him by the blood of the Lamb, and by the word of their testimony; and they loved not their lives unto the death" (Rev. 12:7-11).

The Bible says the saints of old overcame Satan? How? By the "… blood of the Lamb and the word of their testimony." We need to understand that truth, and place ourselves under God's umbrella of protection, through faith in Jesus Christ. We then have the power to command Satan to flee and he will be gone. The Saints overcame by the word of their testimony, coupled with a dedication of their lives to Christ. "They loved not their lives even unto death."

We must dedicate our tongues and our lives to bringing glory and honor to Jesus. The Revival many of us pray for is never going to come until we learn how damaging and destructive the tongue can be and finally and completely dedicate it to Jesus. Mighty Men do that!

Chapter Seven

HOW TO AVOID NEGATIVE THINKING AND ACHIEVE GREATNESS

"The High Jump"

High jumping is a very entertaining sport. I'm always amazed when I see an athlete jump higher than he is tall. Today's elite high jumpers not only exceed their height, but seven feet is also not uncommon.

Seven feet was once considered unachievable, then, on July 27, 1993, Cuba's Javier Sotomayor, set the Olympic record at seven feet, ten inches. Incredibly, some athletes are now jumping over eight feet. Far be it from me to say that no one will ever jump nine feet.

How can we learn to achieve greatness in life and finish at a high level? The high jump gives us many principles that are useful in that pursuit. For instance, how can we raise the standard successfully, reaching our full potential, and then know when it's time to quit?

In 1979, I earned a private pilot's license. I flew all over America, transporting staff and equipment to crusades and rally sites as a full-time, vocational evangelist, for several years. I learned how to fly and, more importantly, how to land. That I was a successful pilot should be self-evident —I'm still alive! There is an old saying: "Flying is the second greatest thrill known to man; landing is the first!"

The truth is, landing an airplane is nothing more than controlling a crash. A pilot begins to throttle back, interspersing power as needed, until the plane safely lands where the pilot intends. We'll return to flying throughout this chapter as both flying and high jumping require overcoming gravity.

Negative thinking is anathema to achieving greatness

Visualize a high jump competition at the Olympic level. The men are jumping a foot or more over their heads. How do they do that? I can assure you they're not indulging in any negative thinking, which limits or denies faith. The great jumpers never approach the bar thinking, "It can't be done."

No one who has ever achieved anything significant started by saying, "It can't be done." People created most of our technological marvels by ignoring the naysayers who said it could not be done. Jesus said, "Without Me, you can do nothing" (John 15:5). Conversely, Paul reminded the Philippian believers that they could accomplish anything that God wanted: "I can do all things through Christ who gives me my strength" (Philippians 4:13).

More negative phrases to avoid

1. "We've never done it that way before."

Those are the last seven words of a dying church. They are the last seven words of any organization or man who embraces such suggestions as well. Mighty Men don't think like that!

2. "We don't have the money."

You may not have the money, but I know someone who does. Scripture reminds us that God owns the cattle on a thousand hills. (God owns the hills too!) There is nothing too big or too hard for God. When we embrace this, there is no limit to how much we can achieve. "We just can't afford that," kills motivation and prevents men from attaining greatness. Mighty Men don't think like that!

3. "Let somebody else do it."

Far too many Christians believe that God's ministry is for someone else because they are either spiritually lazy, or they feel ill-prepared, or feel unworthy. I can empathize with the last group.

Between the time I got serious about my relationship with God, while in college, until I preached my first sermon (about three years later), people would come to me often and say, "I think God is calling you to preach." But I couldn't conceive of myself standing before people and preaching when there were so many things in my life that I was still trying to sort out. However, one day, a light bulb came on, and God gently spoke to me, saying, "Scarborough, if you wait until you're worthy or sinless, you will never preach a sermon and neither would anyone else."

Scripture says that "I may gain Christ and be found in Him, not having a righteousness of my own that comes from the law, but that which is through faith in Christ—the righteousness that comes from God on the basis of faith" (Philippians 3:9). We are fully equipped when our righteousness comes through faith in Christ. Jesus alone makes us worthy. Kingdom work is not someone else's business; it's our business. Me and you. Mighty Men understand that!

4. "I'm too old."

That's what Abraham and Sarah said. So God made them wait another 10 or 12 years before He let them have a baby. He probably did that just to show them, "You haven't seen anything yet." As long as God is on the throne, we are not too old. We might have to alter our methods because of age or other limitations, but God would do so much more through us if we stopped making so many excuses for why He can't use us. Remember, "I can do all things through Christ who gives me strength" (Philippians 4:13). Mighty Men know that!

Three reasons why negative thinking is so damaging

1. Negative thinking stifles creativity.

If we focus on our inability, we're not focused on God's unlimited ability. Where we cannot, God can. Mighty Men believe that!

2. Negative thinking demoralizes others.

A negative attitude affects our associates, neighbors, friends, and family. No one is more miserable to be around than someone who constantly points out all the things that are wrong. Problems are nothing more than opportunities for God. Mighty Men believe that!

3. Negative thinking is depressing.

If we focus solely on our obstacles and inadequacies, we soon find ourselves hopelessly depressed, exuding despair and defeat. I refer to this as getting in a funk.

A funk is how one feels after a solid week of rain, gray clouds, mist, and no sun. After a few days of such weather, we feel gloomy. If we're not careful, we begin living in a spirit of despair just because of the weather. I love flying, because once I get above the clouds, regardless of the weather below, the sun is always shining. We must remind ourselves that the "Son" is always shining, despite the clouds of depression that occasionally overwhelms us. If we keep our eyes on the Son, we will always be hopeful. Mighty Men embrace that!

Begin thinking creatively

To dispel negative thinking, we must quit taking an inventory of our inadequacies and remind ourselves that Jesus is alive and on His throne. We must "take every thought captive and make it obedient to the truth" (2 Corinthians 10:5b). Jesus told us that "with man this is impossible, but with God all things are possible" (Matthew 19:26).

We can achieve at the highest level, just as the high jumpers do, if we look to Jesus, the author and finisher of our faith. Achieving greatness requires creative thinking.

In the early days of high jumping, competitors ran up to the bar, and the jumper with the most spring in his legs jumped the highest. On a good day, they might jump four feet. Eventually, someone said, "There's got to be a better way." Someone discovered that if he lifted one leg up at a time, the sheer motion itself would lift his whole body. The "scissors jump" technique resulted in new records. When I was a high jumper in junior high, that was the method we were taught.

Then someone envisioned a better way—diving headfirst over the bar. After all, as the adage says, where the head goes, the body will follow. Jumpers were soon setting new records.

A great example of creative thinking

In 1968, the track and field world was amazed when Oregon State's Dick Fosbury revealed a whole new method. While everyone else continued to jump the same old way, thinking creatively, he ran up to the bar and, at the last moment, turned and jumped backwards. His first few attempts were unsuccessful, but he kept working at it until he perfected it. In the 1968 Olympics, Dick Fosbury won the Gold Medal, setting a world record with what became known as the "Fosbury Flop."

He proved to the jumping world that by running up to the bar and turning just a little, he could arch his back to get higher, and then by kicking his legs out, he could push on the back end instead of the front end of the jump. Suddenly, 7 feet became doable. Then 7'2," 7'4," 7'10," and finally, someone cleared the unthinkable 8 feet. Incredible, you say? Not with God, for He made man in His image. Like Dick Fosbury, who thought outside the box, Mighty Men can accomplish much IF they allow their Creator to infuse their hearts and minds with His limitless imagination.

Far too often, we limit God to what we know, failing to recognize that He has unlimited ways to solve every problem or challenge we face. We think that what we know is all there is to know, but God's knowledge exceeds our knowledge. Isaiah reminds us, "For my thoughts are not your thoughts, neither are your ways my ways," declares the Lord. "As the heavens are higher than the earth, so are my ways higher than your ways and my thoughts than your thoughts" (Isaiah 55:8-9).

If we allow God to work through us, there is no limit to what He can do. His only limitation is that which we place on Him. To achieve greatness, we need to rely more on God and less on ourselves.

A quick test

Before I go any further, I want to give you a test. Don't panic; you will not be graded. It comes from John C. Maxwell's book, *Developing the Leader Within You.* Take a minute and examine the nine dots below. Connect the nine dots with four straight lines. Now here's the catch—you must do this without lifting your pen or pencil from the paper.

```
•   •   •

•   •   •

•   •   •
```

(Option 1)

Can it be done without adding a fifth line? Perhaps you're now thinking, "It can't be done!" Let me assure you that it is very doable. Maxwell presents six ways to connect those dots, but to do so, you must set aside assumptions that closed your mind. In the first illustration, start at point "A" and follow the arrows and you will see one way it can be done.

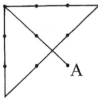

(Option 2)

Very few people get that right because the first thing we do is to look at those dots and put borders on our thinking. Here's the second way. Now that took only three lines. The presumption is that we have to go right through the heart of every dot, but who said that? Just touching them is all we have to do.

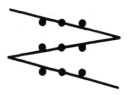

(Option 3)

Let's try another one. We could do it with just one mark—Maxwell challenges his readers with, "Did I define how wide the lines should be? Let's do it again."

(Option 4)

Okay, please visualize this with me. Put these nine dots on a piece of paper. Fold the paper right in the middle between the dots. If we fold it correctly, we can line them up so that all three rows of dots touch, then connect them with just one line.

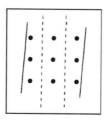

(Option 5)

Here's another idea. Did anybody say we couldn't take the piece of paper and circle it around a pen? If we do that, we can use a spiral and connect it with one line.

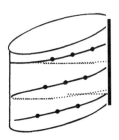

(Option 6)

Another option would be to tear the paper into nine pieces with one dot on each. Then you could connect all the dots by poking a hole through all the dots with your pencil!

There are apparently a lot of ways to do this. The problem is that we freeze ourselves into a way of thinking in the same way we prevent God from showing us life's possibilities. Thus, we don't achieve at the highest level. The men and women who have moved this nation forward, and have changed society for the better, learned how to think outside the lines. Mighty Men learn to think creatively!

Audacity and tenacity

Christopher Columbus was among the greatest creative thinkers of his day. Men of the sea, in his time, believed that the world ended somewhere beyond the horizon. Maps were drawn to reflect that belief. But Columbus believed the world was round, and he chose to ignore existing nautical science. Columbus met significant resistance for his idea to circle the world, but he refused to let go of his dream to achieve greatness.

Over seven long years, he visited heads of state, until King Ferdinand, and Queen Isabella of Spain agreed to underwrite his voyage. Even then, Columbus wasn't satisfied. He demanded to be named the Governor of his discoveries, Captain of the Seas, and be given a percentage of all the treasure he brought back.

Ferdinand and Isabella agreed. The rest is history. America was born. Do we have that kind of audacious faith? Mighty Men do!

Do we have the kind of faith that Orville and Wilbur Wright demonstrated? Despite all the naysayers, these brothers persisted until they succeeded in piloting the first airplane flight on December 17, 1903, at Kitty Hawk, North Carolina. I doubt that even they dreamed that someday we'd be flying, not only around the world, but to the moon. Or that there would be a space telescope, called Hubbell, taking pictures of the universe someday, because two men in 1903 said, "We're not going to listen to those who say we can't." It should be that way for all of us who are in Christ, for Scripture says: "...for everyone born of God overcomes the world. This is the victory that has overcome the world, even our faith" (1 John 5:4). With Christ in us we possess what it takes to ignore naysayers and succeed where others failed. Christ in us enables us to achieve greatness. Mighty Men are like that!

That's the essence of Christianity. That's why a disproportionate share of the significant scientific findings have come from where Christianity has flourished. And the vast majority of those discoveries have come from Mighty Men who unashamedly confessed to a belief in God, such as Galileo, Descartes, Pascal, Newton, Lord Kelvin, Max Planck, and Human Genome Project Director Francis Collins.

"Now faith is being sure of what we hope for and certain of what we cannot see. This is what the ancients were commended for. By faith, we understand that the universe was formed at God's command, so that what is seen was not made with what was visible. By faith, Abel offered God a better sacrifice than Cain did. By faith he was commended as a righteous man when God spoke well of his offering, and by faith he still speaks even though he is dead. By faith Enoch was taken from life so that he did not experience death and he could not be found because God had taken him away. For before he was taken he was commended as one who pleased. And without faith it is impossible to please God because anyone who comes to Him must believe that He exists and that He rewards those who earnestly seek Him" (Hebrews 11:1-6).

Faith, which gives birth to creative thinking, sees the unseeable, solves the unsolvable, and accomplishes the impossible, at the highest level.

Beyond positive thinking

Biblical thinking exceeds the limited philosophy of positive thinking. It's true that just saying, "You can, you can, you can," may help some people achieve more. However, achieving greatness in life involves more than just getting rid of negative thinking; it is learning to think like Christ. That's the key to achieving at the highest level. That's the secret to becoming a Mighty Man.

Developing the mind of Christ within ourselves enables us to attain the right perspective. When a man takes an airplane to 10,000 feet, he may derive great personal satisfaction. He may feel like a pilot. But he still has to land it. If he can't do that, flying is not a great achievement; it's suicide.

I will never forget my first solo flight. Typically, pilots learn to fly in a very simple, fixed-wing aircraft. The Piper Lance, which our ministry purchased before I learned to fly, was a high-performance, complex, six-passenger aircraft with retractable landing gear that cruised at 180 miles per hour. It was not recommended for student pilots because it required much more skill than planes typically used for training.

However, since that was the plane I'd be flying after the lessons, I wanted to learn to fly in it. In relatively routine time my instructor felt I was ready to fly solo. I remember that day so well. I took the Piper Lance up all alone for the first time, flew a while, and then circled the airport and landed. The instructors were all there waiting for me when I walked into the office. They congratulated me and clipped off a portion of my shirt, which is a tradition among pilots when someone solos for the first time, and celebrated my successful flight.

Then I went back out, got in the plane and wrecked it. It wasn't serious. I simply came in too fast and hit on the nose wheel of the plane a little too hard, instead of the two wheels affixed to the wings. It started vibrating violently. By the time I reached the end of the runway and began turning the plane around, the nose-wheel collapsed, causing the propeller to strike the ground. The repairs cost close to $8,000.00, due largely to the fact that the FAA required me to have a certified mechanic go through the entire engine checking for damage. Taking off is relatively easy, but it requires skill to land. My insurance rates were a painful reminder of the importance of landing correctly for the next three years.

Getting the plane off the ground requires full throttle power, which you keep until the plane reaches a safe altitude. Then the pilot can reduce power and level off. Cruising speed uses about 60% or 80% power, depending on the aircraft, allowing the pilot to conserve fuel and get maximum efficiency. If all systems indicate it to be safe, the pilot is then able to engage the autopilot and let the plane fly itself, as he continues to monitor all systems.

Flying is exhilarating!

Built for turbulence

I've often heard people say, "I've flown a plane." However, after a brief discussion, I discerned that most often what they experienced is sitting in the co-pilot seat when the pilot gave them control of the plane (after the plane has been comfortably positioned at cruising altitude). I don't want to deflate anyone's ego, but flying a plane is not hard once it's up there. Many people have had that experience. But that's not truly flying.

The instructors spend most of their training time rehearsing stalls and other emergency procedures so that the student pilot is prepared for every possible situation that might arise while flying. The student must attain competence before being given charge over the aircraft. As I stated earlier, flying is the second greatest thrill known to man—landing is the first!

So, how can we land our plane of life successfully or, better stated, how can we achieve greatness in life? We can only reach it by developing the mind of Christ. This will enable us to live successfully without getting into a crisis that results in a crash. Many people and organizations have flown high, for a season, but crashed in the end.

Unfortunately, when that happens, all that people remember is how it ended. I've never read a newspaper story in which a couple of hundred people died in a plane crash; that elaborated on how pleasant the flight was—before the accident. They never report that during the first two hours, the passengers had a great time. They may have listened to beautiful music, watched a classic movie and eaten a delicious meal, but that does not interest us if the plane crashes.

Life is more than just taking off and sustaining flight. God is interested in the whole picture. The only way we'll be able to keep it all in perspective is to understand what the Bible says about life. To do so, we must spend time in His Word and learn about His ways.

Scripture can put our personal flight in perspective. I get uneasy when I hear people bragging about their achievements, because it is God who gives us the will, and the ability to achieve greatness. (See Philippians 2:13). If we're successful, it's because of God's divine provision. We often fail to recognize how often God's hedge of protection over us comes into play. We should ask ourselves questions like, "Why were we spared when the drunk driver crossed the center median, hit another car, but missed us?" Such questions keep life in perspective. We need to recognize that our lives are protected by grace, and we must develop a spirit of continuous gratitude. We need to realize how interdependent we are with others. Many successful people have lost everything due to events beyond their control. If the stock market collapses, and individuals who owe us money are unable to pay, our businesses could fail as well. We are very interdependent, but if we put ourselves in God's hands and stay in His Word, we will be better equipped to handle success or failure.

Secondly, developing the mind of Christ enables us to understand our purpose in life. God has not given us success so that we can consume it ourselves. We are here for a reason. Have you discovered God's purpose for your life? If you spend time in God's Word, He will reveal His plans and purposes for your life. One thing I'm certain of: we're here to glorify God and point others to Him, not ourselves.

Finally, developing the mind of Christ enables us to finish well. It's not how one starts the flight that matters most; it's how one lands. We have all read stories of those who started off great but, tragically, crashed at the end.

Making course corrections

As a final thought, what about the person who blows it in life? Is it over for him? Absolutely not! Some do not finish as they planned but still finish well because they make significant course corrections during the flight. Most pilots file a flight plan before taking off, but if they encounter an unexpected change in the weather after takeoff, only fools stick with the original flight plan. Wise pilots make course corrections and may even have to pick a different destination for landing if the weather proves too daunting.

Life can throw us a curve ball, but with God, we're never out of the game unless we're unwilling to make the necessary course corrections and wind up crashing. Even then, it is important to remember that God specializes in restoring broken people. It helps me to remember that God did His best work just after a crucifixion.

Two thoughts to consider

1. God wants everyone to achieve greatness.

I believe God wants us to be a success in life. Ethel Waters was right when she testified during Billy Graham crusades, "God don't sponsor no flops." Her English wasn't correct, but her theology was superb. This understanding doesn't necessarily mean we will be wealthy or famous, but God wants us to be the best we can be, using the talents He bestowed on us. God wants us to achieve at the highest level, whether it is sweeping floors or building skyscrapers, making speeches to tens of thousands, or simply talking to our children. God wants us to give our best, and He wants us to allow Him to do His best through us. God wants everyone to achieve greatness.

2. Flying high provides more security than flying low.

In our discussion of how to achieve greatness in life, we've used the analogies of high jumping and flying an airplane. Both have to do with overcoming gravity. When it comes to flying an airplane, why not fly as close to the ground as possible? Would it not require less fuel and allow one to arrive sooner due to less climbing and descending time? Why should one fly high? An airplane is designed for turbulence. A 25-year veteran pilot of a major airline was asked this question during an interview, "Do you ever get fearful when the plane begins to drop in violent, turbulent weather?" He surprisingly answered, "No! It doesn't bother me at all. In fact, most of the severe turbulence is above 25,000 feet. The plane is designed to take turbulence, and it can drop 500 feet or more suddenly on occasion, but the aircraft is designed to handle the stress, and we have plenty of time to recover. The real danger comes when you hit turbulence, rare though it is, and you are less than 5,000 feet off the ground because you may not have time to recover control of the aircraft."

Like an airplane, Mighty Men are designed for turbulence. We can handle more than we think we can. But we have to maintain a safe altitude. We have to get high enough to be assured that we have time to recover when turbulence occurs—and rest assured, in life, there will be turbulence. If we are flying just above the treetops, just barely doing what it takes to get off the ground, when the tough times come, we will probably crash. However, if we've been praying and developing the mind of Christ throughout our lives, then when that violent, turbulent weather comes, all we have to do is keep doing what we've been doing. There will always be time to recover if we are flying high enough when the tough times come.

Elite high jumpers around the world are training every day for competition. Some are experimenting with new techniques, trying to find the next creative way to get an edge. Mighty Men do that too. They continually ask God to stretch their thinking and enlarge their vision so that they can achieve greatness in life. Mighty Men do that.

Chapter Eight

HOW TO GET OFF THE MERRY-GO-ROUND OF LIFE

"The Discus Throw"

Here's a trivia question: What do James Duncan, Eric Krenz, Adolfo Consoline, Jurgen Schult, and Al Oerter (pictured left) have in common?

All of them were world class discus throwers. Most of them were Olympians, who held world records at some point. I've had some experience myself throwing a discus, about which I'll share later.

First, let's meet the real champions. James Duncan of the United States set the first official world record in 1912, with a throw of 47.59 meters, at a track event in Queens, New York. In 1930, Eric Krenz, another American, became the first ever to throw the discus more than 50 meters, with a distance of 51.03 meters, in 1930, at an intercollegiate meet at Palo Alto, California.

Over time, with improved diets and training, men began shattering those records. In 1948, Adolf Consoline of Italy threw the discus more than 55 meters. In 1961, Jay Silvester (USA) cracked the 60-meter barrier with a throw of 60.56 meters.

At that point, people began asking, "Is 70 meters possible?" In 1976, Mac Wilkins (USA) set the world record three times in consecutive throws of 69.80, 70.24 and 70.86 at a meet in San Jose, before winning gold at the Montreal Olympics. Ten years later, current world record holder Jurgen Schult, of Germany, threw it 74.8 meters. He not only surpassed a previous record of 72 meters—he annihilated it.

Until Jurgen Schult, the man with the most durable record for throwing the discus was the previously mentioned James Duncan, who held it for 12 years. Al Oerter of the United States won the Olympic title four consecutive competitions, (1956, 1960, 1964 and 1968).

Unclear on the concept

I mentioned elsewhere how, when I was in ninth grade, the track coach compelled us football players to participate in track and field in order to get our football letter jackets. He assigned us races. I got the quarter mile—440 grueling yards. I hated that race, so I decided to experiment with some field events.

One of those I looked into was the discus throw. The discus is a hardwood platter rimmed with metal. It is 8.63-8.75 inches across and 1.75-1.88 inches thick and weighs 4 pounds, 6.547 ounces. (These are the specifications for men's competitions.)

The idea is to hold the discus flat against the palm and forearm, then whirl around rapidly and propel the discus outward with a whipping motion. The throw must take place within a circle approximately eight feet in diameter. Two straight lines extend from the center of the circle at a 90-degree angle, and all legal throws must land in the area out in the field between these lines.

I had difficulty just picking up the discus. Once you have the right grip, you spin round and round and at the precise moment, with your body in full circular motion, you release it. When done with precision, the discus glides through the air and lands somewhere within the legal limits.

I had a real problem with this concept. After about two turns around, I couldn't remember where I'd started. I threw it at a building. I threw it straight up in the air. I threw it at fellow competitors and coaches, who were forced to duck or die. Once or twice, I threw it right into the ground. I found that I could not make all the parts of my body coordinate so that I could let go at precisely the right moment. It wasn't just that I was terrible at the discus throw—I was dangerous! I never had a clue where it was going. Needless to say, my discus throwing career was short lived.

My experience with the discus throw resembles the way a lot of people are living today—clueless! As adults, we find ourselves spinning round and round, trying to determine how to manage a successful life. There are not many who can be like Al Oerter, who knew how to launch the discus at the precise moment to achieve a world record.

What is the meaning of life?

According to Scripture, the wisest man who ever lived was King Solomon, son of David and the third king of Israel. But even though he was brilliant, he failed to follow his own sage advice in the end. In Ecclesiastes, Solomon laments: "'Meaningless! Meaningless!' says the Teacher. 'Utterly meaningless! Everything is meaningless.' What does man gain from all his labor at which he toils under the sun? Generations come, and generations go, but the earth remains forever" (Eccl. 1:2-4). Solomon further inquired, "What is the meaning of it all?"

Sooner or later, most men come to a place in life where they ask the question, "What is the purpose of life? Where do I fit in all of this?"

Significance

Have you asked that question lately? I suspect that most men, if not all who read this book, have a single great ambition. You can write it down in one long, but meaningful word—Significance.

There is not a person on the planet who is not searching, in one way or another, to find his significance. No one wants to die and be forgotten. That is why most men want headstones on their graves, or erect monuments, or leave vast sums of money, to assure that someone puts their names on buildings.

Wanting to be significant isn't bad, but I've got sobering news! According to God's Word... "No one remembers the former generations, and even those yet to come will not be remembered by those who follow them" (Ecclesiastes 1:11).

Solomon was a man who didn't just dream of doing things. He had the means to experience whatever his heart desired. And he did. But when he wrote his memoirs he said, in effect, "Hey, what is the meaning of it all?"

What's it all about? Solomon said, even men with great names will be forgotten by succeeding generations. We want to be remembered and make our time on this earth meaningful, but we must avoid Satan's great deception if we are to become Mighty Men.

Throughout our lives, we hear deceptive voices lying to us about what constitutes a meaningful life. Madison Avenue has discovered that even though we may resist external temptation, when it comes to buying products, our subconscious retains every message they send across the airwaves or plaster on billboards. Hence, merchants spend millions and millions of advertising dollars trying to brainwash us.

By the time a boy reaches manhood in America, he has seen thousands of images of what Madison Avenue promotes as a successful, happy, and well-adjusted adult. Even those of us who work hard to keep our thoughts pure and Christ-centered are susceptible to these subtle advertising techniques.

In 1973, the movie *The Exorcist* was released. It was an overnight sensation, breaking box office records for a horror film. Although it was scary enough, the producers inserted subliminal images of a demon to induce even greater feelings of terror. One filmgoer, in 1974, sued Warner Brothers, claiming subliminal imagery had made him faint and hit his head on the seat in front of him. The studio settled out of court.

In the 1950s, researchers found that if advertisers planted an image in a movie frame, periodically, that said, "buy popcorn, buy a coke, buy candy," the theater would sell more of these products. This technique, which works best when the suggestion is something a person already wants, was banned as unethical. But it reminds us that our subconscious is buying even when the conscious mind is not. To avoid manipulation, we must be on guard.

Raising expectations

Many have bought into the lie that you have to live a certain way, look a certain way, and do certain things, to find happiness. I remember visiting relatives in Kentucky in 1959, when I was nine years old, and discovering that they had an outhouse —which they used! I couldn't believe it. Then, in the late '70s, I took my kids to my parents' home where I grew up, and they had the same reaction about the house having only a single bathroom. They couldn't believe that a whole family could live with only one bathroom!

Each new generation learns to demand things that the previous generation didn't even know existed. Homes built 40 years ago often had only two to three bedrooms, one bath, a one-car garage or carport, no central air or heat, often no attic fans, and very simple cabinetry. Homes could be built the same way today and be quite affordable, but no one would want them. New single-family homes, at a minimum, have two and a half baths, two to three thousand square feet, a two-car garage, central heat and air.

I was at an airport recently, and two things became quite evident to me. First, everyone was in a hurry. The second thing I noticed was that the world has a lot of funny-looking people (myself included)!

Where are all the beautiful people we see on television and in movies? You know, the ones making those exercise commercials, who have perfect bodies, perfect hair, etc. Where do they live? Where do they work? I've been to the beach, and they're not there either.

My point is, if you watch television too much, you can be deceived into thinking everyone but you has his stuff together. It's easy to get caught up in the rat race of trying to be "somebody." Unfortunately, we end up as I did when trying to master the discus throw. We go round and round and round, being dangerous rather than effective.

The merry-go-round trap

The rat race many call life, reminds me of one of those old-fashioned merry-go-rounds like I grew up with, that could be found in just about every community park. They were big, heavy, metal rigs that floated on ball bearings. It took a pretty strong person to get them started because the inertia was so great. But once you got them going, they were even harder to stop.

Occasionally, the neighborhood bully, or perhaps a well-intended parent, would stand alongside and spin it as fast as they could while children hung on for dear life. No matter how bad you wanted off, you were stuck. If you let go, the momentum would hurl you across the playground. What seemed fun at first, became something of a nightmare.

When our youngest daughter, Kathryn, was about six, we went to the county fair in Mobile, Alabama. It was one of the biggest events in the county each year. This time, they had a brand new ride—a pendulum—that rocked back and forth until it went all the way over the top and started making a 360-degree rotation. That was bad enough, but the compartment you rode in spun round and round as well, making for a deliriously fun thrill ride—at first. My two oldest children had already taken enough of these thrill rides with me. They didn't trust my assurances that it would be "so much fun." But Kathryn was young and innocent, and she had complete confidence in her Daddy.

We were so excited that we giggled as we got into that little box and they strapped us in and put the shoulder harness down. I remember looking at my wife and the other two children while Kathryn and I taunted them. "Hey, you bunch of chickens!" We let them have it. We were having a blast as the ride went back and forth. It went higher and higher and every time we passed the family, we clucked and hollered, "Chicken!"

But then as the ride finally went over the apex and made its first loop and started spinning simultaneously, we quit hollering at them. Now it was about survival. We were going so fast that I had difficulty lifting my head off the backrest. If we moved any part of our bodies, it was hard to bring it back to the original position due to centrifugal force. It was incredible!

I looked over at my little daughter, who wasn't quite tall enough to get on the ride in the first place, and noticed her head pinned against her chest. So I took my hand and forced it back up. She looked at me, pale as a ghost, and said, "Daddy, I'm going to vomit!"

I began imagining what would happen if she did lose it in this small space spinning round and round, and it wasn't pleasant. So with all the authority I could muster, I declared, "No, You Are Not!" Then I prepared myself just in case my faith wasn't adequate, or the Lord had a different plan. The good news is, she held on. I will never forget how relieved I was when the ride finally stopped. We got out, glad to be alive. Instead of our taunting them, the rest of the family began taunting us. And they did so, again and again, for many years.

So much of our pursuit for significance is like those two merry-go-round experiences. We find ourselves saying, "How do I get off?" I've met far too many men who have well-paying jobs with big mortgages on gorgeous homes in the best part of town, but no time to enjoy the home or their families because they have buried themselves in debt. Like Solomon, they spin around and around, saying, "Meaningless! Meaningless! All is meaningless!"

The inordinate pursuit of significance has led many men to great despair and, ultimately, great disaster including broken homes, broken marriages, broken lives, and broken children. Men are competitive by nature, and the quest for significance can lead a person to be suspicious of everyone and everything, especially in the workplace where he's always competing to be the best. How do we get off this merry-go-round?

I learned several things that apply to life while I was a child trying to get off the merry-go-round in the park.

The first thing I learned, while coping with the merry-go-round, was to focus on something stable. While I was going around and around, with my lunch rising in my throat, I discovered that if I did nothing, I'd get sick. But if I focused on the middle post of the merry-go-round, which was the only stationary thing in view, I could hang on till the end.

If you're on the merry-go-round of life and feel like you're about to be thrown off, put your eyes on the only thing that is always the same —Jesus. The Bible says, "He is the same yesterday, today and forever" (Hebrews 13:8).

We live in an ever-changing world, but Jesus Christ is always the same. Get into God's Word. It has hope for today. It will reveal who you are, where you're headed, and will give you principles to assist in finding real significance. Romans 15:4 tells us, "Everything that was written in the past was written to teach us, so that through the endurance taught in the Scriptures and the encouragement they provide we might have hope." God has a design for our lives that does not change, even as circumstances do. Focus on Jesus; He alone is always the same.

Make a decision to get off the merry-go-round permanently.

Getting off sometimes requires a process. It may take some time, depending on how long you've been on the merry-go-round. Life becomes more complicated with age. It probably took you a while, perhaps years, to get into the mess you're in. It may also take a while to get things back on track. But it begins with the decision to change. If you make the decision, God will empower you to be successful, and I can assure you it is worth it. Mighty Men make the changes!

When I was young, I developed a technique for getting off the merry-go-round. First, I'd put one foot over the side and start to drag it. If someone was spinning the merry-go-round, this additional drag would make his task much harder, often resulting in them losing interest in trying to terrorize us kids, and they'd stop.

There is some cost to dragging your foot to slow the momentum. The right toe on my right foot shoe seemed to be the very first part of the shoe to wear out, which never pleased Mom and Dad. But for me, the benefit more than offset the cost.

Many men get caught up in their hobbies, whether it's fishing or golf or some other attraction. In time, even their hobbies can become a merry-go-round, but they feel they can't afford to quit. If you can relate, ask yourself if lowering your handicap is worth losing your wife or kids. I meet men who can't find time for church or afford to tithe, but can afford an expensive bass boat and enter fishing tournaments several weekends a year—which means perfecting their craft on most of the rest of the weekends. There's nothing wrong with fishing or golf, but Mighty Men have to make choices.

Beginning the process of letting go

To get off the merry-go-round of life, you must be willing to admit, "I need help!" And, you have to start the process. As you focus on Christ, life takes on new meaning. As you get into His Word, you reevaluate what's significant and what is not. As you align your views with God's Word, you begin to reprioritize. You don't have to do this on your own, nor should you. In fact, God's Word tells us, "When we cry out to Him, He answers and makes us bold and gives us strength of soul" (Psalm 138:3). We simply have to cry out.

Perhaps right now, you're sensing a need to stop and ask Him to show you how to slow down the merry-go-round. I can assure you that if you ask Him how to bring balance back into your life, He will. James 1:5 says, "If any of you lacks wisdom, he should ask God, who gives generously to all without finding fault."

Make Jesus Lord of your life. As the merry-go-round slowed down on the playground to a safe speed, I jumped off. You have to be the judge as to when you can survive the jump, but jump you must. You have to plant both feet on the ground and say, "That's enough!" One thing I've learned is that I can't change you or anyone else. And, when things are spinning out of control, I can't change me. But I can call on Jesus and IF I do my part, He will do His.

The time will come when you can say, "I'm not playing this game any longer," because nobody survives the merry-go-round. Ecclesiastes 12 draws a conclusion to the false search for significance. Ask yourself, "Where am I in life? Where do I want to get? How do I get there?" Don't stay trapped on the merry-go-round, rather, with God's help, develop a plan of action. Then, execute the plan. From time to time, you'll need to evaluate the results and refine the process. Though the message of Christ never changes, the methods often do. Ecclesiastes 12:13-14 says, "Now all has been heard; here is the conclusion of the matter: Fear God and keep his commandments, for this is the whole duty of man. For God will bring every deed into judgment, including every hidden thing, whether it is good or evil."

This is the best advice I can give for getting off the merry-go-round and honing your spiritual discus throwing skills. To be able to spin around and let go at the precise moment to land within the boundaries, you must learn to fear God and keep His commandments.

Sooner or later, everyone who gets on the merry-go-round is sickened by it. No one is exempt. "Be not deceived; God is not mocked: for whatsoever a man soweth, that shall he also reap. For he that soweth to his flesh shall of the flesh reap corruption; but he that soweth to the Spirit shall of the Spirit reap life everlasting" (Galatians 6:7-8).

Rest assured; you will get off the merry-go-round. You have a choice, either put a foot down, dragging it until you're comfortable stopping the merry-go-round, or wait until you are thrown off when you least expect it. But you ARE going to get off.

Jesus alone can make life worth living. John 10:10 says, "The thief comes only to steal and kill and destroy;" but Jesus said, "I have come that you might have life and have it to the full." Jesus is the solution for those of us who are on the merry-go-round. To every generation he offers the same solution: "Come to me all you who are weary and burdened and I will give you rest" (Matthew 11:28).

If you are a person who has never met Christ as your personal Savior, the first step in getting off the merry-go-round is to let Him have first place in your heart. The world inundates us with wrong messages, and it's easy to lose our way. Jesus said, "I am the way and the truth and the life. No one comes to the Father except through me" (John 14:6).

If you know Jesus as your personal Savior, but as you read this chapter you realize you've gotten off track, the answer is—Get back to Jesus. If you're frustrated—if you're tired of trying to survive the merry-go-round, then ask for God's help. Resolve to take the steps to make Jesus the Lord of your life once again. If you do your part, I KNOW He will do His part. Mighty Men get that!

Chapter Nine

HOW TO PUSH
THROUGH OBSTACLES

"The Shot Put"

Few people recognized the name of Randy Barnes when he won the silver medal in the shot put at the 1988 Olympics in Seoul, Korea. In 1989, he set the world indoor record by throwing it 74 feet, 4.25 inches. In 1990, he set the outdoor world record of 75 feet, 10.25 inches.

At the 1996 Summer Olympics in Atlanta, everyone who followed track and field knew who Randy Barnes was. He won Olympic gold by throwing the shot put 70 feet, 11.25 inches.

What makes Randy Barnes' feat so remarkable is what he was throwing. At first glance, it may not look like much to us, but the shot put weighs 16 pounds, about as much as one of the heavier bowling balls. The only way I could throw the shot put as far as an Olympic athlete would be if I stood on top of a seven-story building and dropped it. The power and strength of these athletes are simply astounding.

While I was the senior pastor at a church in Pearland, Texas, southeast of Houston, one of our associate pastors lead a young high school athlete named George Paraskevopoulous to Christ. George was a senior at Pearland High School, and one of the top high school shot putters in Texas. He led all competitors in our area and had already pushed the shot 57 feet, 7 inches. His coach, John Morris, told me that not only was George naturally gifted, but he was also one of the most mentally tough athletes he had ever coached.

In Philippians 3:12-14 we read, "Not that I have already obtained all this or have already been made perfect, but I press on to take hold of that for which Christ Jesus took hold of me. Brothers, I do not consider myself yet to have taken hold of it. But this one thing I do: Forgetting what is behind and straining toward what is ahead, I press on toward the goal to win the prize for which God has called me heavenward in Christ Jesus."

Two keys to success

In the face of various obstacles each day, how do we press on toward the goal to win the prize for which God has called us?

Coach Morris once told me that there were two keys to success in the shot put: strength and technique. Although some of us are born naturally stronger than others, the power that Randy Barnes exhibited when he threw the shot over 70 feet was not accidental. He didn't get stronger by wishing it, but rather by working out hard every day. Similarly, Christians do not get stronger by accident. We must work hard at building our faith in Christ.

Scriptures exhort us to be strong. Sadly, most men who attend church today are weak-willed and spiritually immature. Using the battle-outfitted Roman soldier as a metaphor, Paul exhorts us in Ephesians 6:10-18:

> Finally, be strong in the Lord and in his mighty power. Put on the full armor of God, so that you can take your stand against the devil's schemes. For our struggle is not against flesh and blood, but against the rulers, against the authorities, against the powers of this dark world and against the spiritual forces of evil in the heavenly realms. Therefore put on the full armor of God, so that when the day of evil comes, you may be able to stand your ground, and after you have done everything, to stand. Stand firm then, with the belt of truth buckled around

your waist, with the breastplate of righteousness in place, and with your feet fitted with the readiness that comes from the gospel of peace. In addition to all this, take up the shield of faith, with which you can extinguish all the flaming arrows of the evil one. Take the helmet of salvation and the sword of the Spirit, which is the word of God. And pray in the Spirit on all occasions with all kinds of prayers and requests. With this in mind, be alert and always keep on praying for all the Lord's people.

Let's review what the armor of God involves:

1. The belt of truth;

2. The breastplate of righteousness;

3. The shoes of the gospel of peace;

4. The shield of faith;

5. The helmet of salvation;

6. The sword of the Spirit.

Why are we to wear this armor? "So that when the day of evil comes, you may be able to stand your ground, and after you have done everything, to stand" (Ephesians 6:13).

In John 3:6, our Lord said, "Flesh gives birth to flesh, the Spirit gives birth to spirit." Therefore, if we are strong in the Lord, it is by design—God's design and our own. We must study God's Word and apply it daily. Our faithfulness determines the level of our strength in putting on the whole armor of God and practicing truth, righteousness, peace, faith, salvation and living in the Spirit.

Overcoming cultural indoctrination

Unfortunately, we live in a world full of shortcuts. Though we might be tempted to try them to thwart obstacles that Satan puts in our path, we soon realize that they don't work. The Apostle Paul exhorted us to be strong. Spiritually weak men cannot survive and stand up against today's increasingly pagan culture. Men must be Mighty to prevail!

Growing stronger requires self-denial. I wonder how many times George Paraskevopoulous faced the choice of going out with friends or going to the field house to train? Because he was willing to pay the price of training for years while other students were partying, George received statewide acclaim and scholarship offers from major universities across the country.

We live in a culture that believes self-denial is foolish. When was the last time you denied yourself something you desired, for a greater good? I'm not talking about things we deny ourselves because we can't afford them. I denied myself a Harley Davidson motorcycle for years because I didn't have the money. I'm talking about those things within our grasp that we willingly choose to ignore for a greater good. Anyone who holds down a job does this every day, but we're thinking about more significant denial and greater reward than mere survival.

Paul describes this type of self-denial in Ephesians 4:22-24: "You were taught, with regard to your former way of life, to put off your old self, which is being corrupted by its deceitful desires; to be made new in the attitude of your minds; and to put on the new self, created to be like God in true righteousness and holiness."

When was the last time you fasted for a day, week or longer because you wanted to seek God and grow stronger in your faith? When was the last time you said no to self-indulgence? When was the last time you avoided a movie that you wanted to see because you knew there was something in it that would displease our Lord? We grow stronger spiritually through self-denial. But we can't grow stronger spiritually until we develop the strength to say no to the temptations of this world and yes to the things of Christ. When we feed our flesh, the carnal desires of our flesh grow stronger. If we feed our spirit by reading God's Word and doing His will, our spirit becomes stronger. Remember, we are not doing this on our own. Mighty Men know that.

Jesus said, "If any man would come after me, he must deny himself and take up his cross daily and follow me" (Luke 9:23). Why did He say that? The answer is clear. The cross is an instrument of death. We must be willing to die to self. Why daily? For the faithful follower of Jesus, every day brings hard choices. In every area of life, Mighty Men choose self-denial to please our Lord and seek His help to accomplish it.

Feeding the baby Christians

Growing stronger also requires a proper diet. The Bible says, "Anyone who lives on milk, being still an infant, is not acquainted with the teaching about righteousness. But solid food is for the mature, who by constant use have trained themselves to distinguish between good and evil" (Hebrews 5:13-14).

In 1 Corinthians 3:1-3, Paul wrote, "I could not address you as spiritual but as worldly—mere infants in Christ. I gave you milk, not solid food, for you are still not ready. You are still worldly. For since there is jealousy and quarreling among you, are you not worldly?"

Tragically, far too many Christians, having been saved by faith, have not lived by faith, and have resisted God's leading them toward maturity. They remain babes in the faith, requiring continual nurturing rather than ministering to others.

If we are going to get past such childish behavior and become the Mighty Men our nation needs to survive, we must do what is necessary to grow stronger in our faith. It will take self-denial, it will take digging into the meat of God's Word and it will take living it.

Mr. Paraskevopoulous and Mr. Barnes did not become shot put champions by eating anything they wanted. Many of us consume hours of television and very little meat from God's Word. What did your spiritual diet consist of this week? Are you spending time in God's Word? Are you applying God's Word daily and thus exercising your spiritual muscles to make your faith stronger? As we push through obstacles in life, we must remember that every challenge prepares us for bigger ones down the road. Psalm 84:5,7 says, "Blessed is the man whose strength is in You, whose heart is set on pilgrimage. They go from strength to strength, until they each appear before God in Zion."

I have learned that when I stay active and maintain a disciplined exercise regimen, it improves my ability to think and concentrate. When I was younger, that regime included running up to five miles a day at a good clip. Now that I'm older, and can't run at the same clip, I watch what I eat and exercise regularly. Exercise increases the flow of blood to the brain and heart and enables us to accomplish more, live longer and feel better. This disciplined lifestyle is also true spiritually.

Living Supernaturally

What do you do when someone offends or harms you? When someone wrongs us, it's natural to want to get even. But with Christ's help, we can choose to live supernaturally and exercise forgiveness, remembering that we have offended Christ, and He has forgiven us. That doesn't mean we become someone's doormat; it means we want to move from the milk of God's Word into the meat of God's Word. By doing so, we grow stronger.

As followers of Christ, we have the liberty to hold a grudge against those who do us wrong, but we also have the opportunity to exercise the forgiveness which makes us spiritually stronger and liberates us from the bondage of the grudge we held. The same is true with prayer. We can choose to pray or not to pray. God enriches our prayer life when we pray, and our spirit grows stronger as well.

We can watch television and open our minds to suggestion, or we can exercise our minds by reading our Bibles and other edifying books and receive a sense of peace that only God can provide. We can look and lust or choose to say no and grow. We can get up and go to church and apply ourselves while there, or we can stay home and grow spiritually fat and lazy. Mighty Men exercise their faith regularly.

Champion athletes, like George and Randy, become renowned through exercise, self-denial, and proper diet. Likewise, Christians become healthy through exercise, self-denial, and a nutritional diet. As I said, there are no shortcuts. Going to church for years will not make us strong Christians any more than putting our names down on a shot put team will make us champions in the shot put. Many people in the church think that a title and tenure equate to spiritual power and might. "I've been here for 'x' number of years, and I've served in 'x' positions over the years; therefore I have rights," they surmise. God's Word makes it clear that tenure and rank make us no more spiritually mature than sitting in our garages for 25 years would make us a Shelby Cobra. Mighty Men recognize that!

According to Coach Morris, George was a success in the shot put, not just because he was strong, but because he had the best technique that he had ever seen in a high school athlete. "To be a good shot putter," the coach explained, "you've got to develop coordination, quickness, control and timing."

The real meaning of meekness

The strongest athlete in the school may not necessarily win the shot put. Why? Because he must first learn to coordinate all of that strength, bringing it under control. The Bible has a good word for this. It is "meekness." Jesus said, "... the meek will inherit the earth" (Matthew 5:5). Meekness is strength—raw, brute strength—under control.

An Olympic shot putter trains daily and disciplines himself. He enters a seven-foot circle and picks up the 16-pound shot, positions it on the fingers of the throwing hand, and rests the hand against his shoulder with the shot under his chin. Then, with his mind and strength focused, he begins to bound or hop across the circle in a half crouch, turning and building speed as he goes. At precisely the right moment, as he reaches the other side of the ring, he faces forward, straightens and puts the shot with an explosive, uncoiling of the arm and body. Ultimately, he hopes to hear an eruption from the crowd as he sets a new world record or wins an Olympic gold medal. After 12 years of disciplined training, Randy Barnes won his gold because he learned how to harness his power and strength and unleash it under control. That illustrates meekness. Mighty Men are Meek Men!

A proper technique takes perfect timing and coordination. Had Randy crossed the line of the circle as he launched the shot 70 feet, the throw would have been disallowed. He had to come just short of the line, but not too short or else forfeit some length.

Many times, in our Christian walk, we do all the right things, but because our timing is not God's timing, it proves unproductive or even counterproductive. Many times, I've regretted saying the right thing at the wrong time.

For me, living in the Spirit is a lot like playing golf. There's a lot to remember. Just about the time I learn how to putt straight, I forget how fast to putt and roll the ball eight feet past the hole. I just can't seem to remember it all at the same time. I tee the ball and drive it a mile, but it goes out of bounds. There's a lot to remember.

Walking in the Spirit is similar because there is so much involved. The only way to get it right is to rely entirely on Christ. We cannot do it without Him. The Good News is that we are not expected to do it without Him.

Pushing through obstacles is not just saying the right thing or doing the right thing. It is not just ingesting the proper diet or exercising regularly. The timing must also be right. Jesus gave us the key when He stated, "Whatever the Father does, the Son also does" (John 5:19). In essence, He learned to stay in touch, and in tune, with His Father. If we are to do that, then we must spend time with Him in His Word and in prayer. Jesus said, "Abide in Me, and I in you. As the branch cannot bear fruit of itself unless it abides in the vine, so neither can you unless you abide in Me" (John 15:4).

Developing mental toughness

Earlier, I indicated that Coach Morris commended George most for his mental toughness. This character trait is so vital if we are to overcome the obstacles we face, and ultimately obtain our prize at the finish line. We too must develop it.

When I think of mental toughness, I think of the men and women who have served in our armed forces in times of war. Homesickness can be a major obstacle to effectiveness when one is stationed in a combat zone far from home with little or no means of communication with the family. A soldier doesn't do what he feels like doing; he does what he's told to do. Mental toughness is required.

I had a church member, who served in the military overseas, tell me that he didn't get to see his son until the child was 18 months old. Some men never get to see their kids because they give their lives in combat. It takes mental toughness to be a good soldier and fight a war.

We must recognize that we're in a war for the soul of our nation. To win against evil, we must develop strong minds so we can do the right thing rather than what may feel good at the time.

I've been advised over and over to keep my sermons positive: "People do not want to go to church to hear reality." Many go to church to feel good. In fact, Scripture warned that this would happen, "For the time will come when men will not tolerate sound doctrine, but with itching ears, they will gather around themselves teachers to suit their own desires" (2 Timothy 4:3). But we can't afford the luxury of sitting around feeling good while Satan and his legions are trying to snuff out every vestige of Christianity. More Christians are being persecuted today around the world than at any time in history, and most church members don't want to hear about and or do anything about it. Shame on us.

In 2015, I was invited, along with several other Christian leaders, to address the United Nations on Christian persecution around the world. I studied the issue carefully and was overwhelmed to learn how many followers of Jesus are losing their lives while the world and even most of Christendom looks the other way. We were all shocked to witness 12 Christians, including one 12-year-old boy, defiantly shout the name of Jesus as ISIS terrorists cut off their heads in Syria on August 28, 2015.

But Christian martyrdom is not just happening in Middle Eastern countries. I remember vividly the images broadcast around the world in 1999, as the two murderous students in Aurora, Colorado, roamed the halls of Columbine High School with military style weapons, terrorizing and shooting fellow students before turning their guns on themselves. Later, we discovered they were Satanists, and that they killed many of their victims because they would not recant their Christian faith. In Oregon, nine students were shot in October of 2015, as the gunman sought out Christians to execute.

The blessing and curse of technology

Now, more than ever, followers of Christ need to develop the tough, disciplined mind of a good soldier and put on the full armor of Christ. Technology that would enable the government to monitor our every activity is no longer science fiction. Pet owners have GPS chips implanted so that satellites can locate the animal if lost. A growing number of people are using similar technology to protect loved ones who have Alzheimer's. What a great innovation—who would want his parents to be lost?

Some well-meaning but short-sighted activists are now advocating for children to be tagged to protect against predators. The uses for such a device are endless. Interpol could track an international terrorist when he walks through the airport scanner. Every piece of currency could be marked to make tracking drug money much simpler.

All of these innovations remind me of a sobering observation by C.S. Lewis that every power gained by man is also a power over man. The Scriptures warn us that in the last days, a world dictator will arise who will require every person on earth to accept the "mark of the beast" in order to acquire food. (See Revelation 13:16-17.) No one knows when those days will arrive, but those who would live in such an age must become spiritually informed and mentally tough. We can do that by dedicating ourselves to becoming active in our faith and more knowledgeable of our Lord and His ways.

Throwing the shot put is an individual sport and, in a real sense, so is Christianity. The shot putter is a member of the track team, but when he gets in the circle, he enters it alone. We are part of the body of Christ, and there is power when two or three gather together. But deep in our souls, when we get in the circle with our enemy the devil, only Jesus can get in there with us. We must wear the armor of God and walk with Christ if our goal is to win. "In all these things we are more than conquerors through Him who loved us" (Romans 8:38). Mighty Men win!

A winning game plan

As we push through obstacles, we need to remind ourselves that things will arise that are beyond our control. When a spouse walks out the door and says, "I'm not coming back," the innocent victim of divorce cannot make them stay. They may not like it, and it may break their hearts, but things happen in life over which we have no control. When a child goes his or her way and rejects the teachings of godly parents, the mother and father are heartbroken. But the reality is that they cannot make a choice for that child once the child reaches a certain age. However, starting with a consistent prayer life, there is so much that we can control—and we should focus on those things.

We must become active members of a local, Bible-centered and teaching church. Bible study classes can help us learn the deeper truths of God. We can feed and nourish our children's hearts with godly principles from Scripture. We can personally seek God's will in everything we do. And, most importantly, we can avail ourselves of the most powerful means of effecting change—prayer.

When Nehemiah began building the wall around Jerusalem, it was with a broken heart but a steely resolve. In one hand he held the implements of repair and in the other he held a sword. What a lesson for us. We must repair what we can and equip ourselves for spiritual warfare at the same time.

Finally, we need to recognize that the real battle is in the mind. The Bible cautions us, saying, "Set your mind on things above, not on earthly things. Put to death therefore whatever belonged to your earthly nature" (Colossians 3:2,5). This mindset is akin to saying, "Garbage In, Garbage Out." If we feed the flesh, temptations of the flesh will grow. If we feed the spirit, the spirit will grow. Mighty Men feed the spirit!

What obstacles are you facing today? What roadblocks are in your way? There is only one sure way to push through the obstacles—"be strong in the Lord and in His mighty power" (Ephesians 6:10). To grow stronger, we must deny self, exercise spiritually and feast on the meat of God's Word. As we build our spiritual strength, we must yield it to the control and power of Jesus, who will enable us to push through all obstacles and become Mighty Men.

Jesus faced many obstacles in His short life on earth. He was persecuted and arrested. He was beaten and mocked. And when they put Him in the tomb, and covered the entrance with a stone and guarded it with soldiers, He pushed the stone away and pushed through the last great obstacle—death. "For everyone born of God overcomes the world. This is the victory that has overcome the world, even our faith" (1 John 5:4). Mighty Men possess overcoming faith!

Chapter Ten

HOW TO
OVERCOME FEAR

"The 400-Meter Run"

In the early '70s, *Chariots of Fire* was released. I don't often recommend a motion picture made in Hollywood because even the best movies tend to compromise our values at some point. But *Chariots of Fire* is an exception.

I remember how this true story impacted those who saw it. It also won over the critics and the Motion Picture Academy, which awarded it the Oscar for Best Picture. The movie depicted part of the life of Olympic athlete Eric Liddell, who later served as a missionary to China, where he died a martyr for his faith in 1945.

Mr. Liddell was a famous rugby player in Scotland, known to his fans as the "Flying Scot," due to his unequaled speed. He also excelled in track, particularly in the 100-meter sprint. Eric Liddell was a committed Christian, reared in a family of missionaries. To the dismay of some in his missionary family, he decided to delay his voyage to China and his life's work as a missionary to try out for the United Kingdom's Olympic team in 1924. He made the team in the 100-meter and 200-meter sprints along with one other sprinter, England's champion, Harold Abrahams.

Paris, France hosted the 1924 Olympic Games. When they announced the schedule for the 100-meter Prelims, Eric was crestfallen. His hope of winning a gold medal for his country was dashed. His qualifying heat was scheduled for Sunday, and Eric had a well known religious conviction that he should not compete on the Sunday Sabbath. Neither his coaches nor teammates could shake him from his belief that Sunday was for God alone. When news of his decision became public—that he refused to run the race, for which he had trained for months—his countrymen were angered and felt betrayed. In one of the movie's most powerful scenes, politicians and even a Royal Family member pressured the young man to run until he stood up and exclaimed, "I won't do this!"

Crafting a solution

When it became apparent that Eric wouldn't budge, a compromise was offered and approved by the governing body of the Olympics. He was given an opportunity to enter the 400-meter run in which he hadn't trained, but humbly accepted. On the Sunday of the qualifiers for the 100 meters, Eric Liddell shared his faith with a group of churchmen and visitors, using his fame as an athlete as a platform to draw fans to hear the Gospel, all for the glory of God. Mighty Men do that!

The whole world was watching on the day of the 100-meter race, and Harold Abrahams, whom Eric Liddell had beaten several times in earlier competitions, won the gold medal. From the world's secular vantage point, Liddell forfeited an almost certain gold medal for his faith. But then he ran the 400-meter race. Eric shocked the world by not only winning the gold medal but by setting new Olympic and world records with a time of 47.6 seconds. Mighty Men honor God, and God honors Mighty Men!

The 1924 Olympics were kind to Eric, as he also competed in the 200-meter finals, in which he won the bronze medal behind Americans Jackson Scholz and Charles Paddock, and beat his British rival and teammate Harold Abrahams, who finished in sixth place. God reminds us: Those who honor me I will honor, but those who despise me will be disdained" (1 Samuel 2:30). God honored Eric Liddell. It took a tremendous amount of courage for Eric to endure the doubts and insults of his king, countrymen, and fellow athletes to fulfill his promise to God that he would never compete on Sundays. But that's the kind of courage that God requires of all his followers. We must overcome fear in order to succeed. We have to be willing to take risks in life to discover for ourselves that God, plus no one, is a majority. Mighty Men know that!

Can you imagine how Eric's heart was pounding as he crouched, waiting for the starter's gun in the 400 meters, flanked by the best runners in the world? Was God pleased? Long after Eric died in China, his testimony still inspires people today. Many runners have since surpassed Eric's record, but none has inspired more people. Eric Liddell faced all of his fears and discovered that God was sufficient. He WAS a Mighty Man!

Facing the ultimate challenge

Every man must work out his salvation in fear and trembling before the Lord. I don't want to debate whether or not a person can work or run on Sunday. The real question for us all is whether we have the moral fortitude to keep our commitments. Are we willing to suffer for our faith? Eric settled that issue once and for all in 1924 in Paris, and when he was faced with death or denial years later in China he was ready. As the Communists started killing Christians by the tens of thousands, Eric stood firmly in his faith. He had faced his fears head on years earlier. Have you faced your fears?

Most men in the church allow their fears to prevent them from being all that they could be. Christian author, Michael Pritchard, observes, "Fear is that dark little room where negatives are developed." For my generation, which came up before everyone on the planet carried an instant camera in their phones, that's a vivid word picture. There was a time when developing a photo required a lengthy chemical process in the darkroom. Pritchard reminds us that there's a darkroom in our minds where the evil one will use our imaginations to develop fear if we're not vigilant.

When size doesn't matter

Fran Tarkenton was the Minnesota Vikings' quarterback throughout the '60s and '70s. He was known for his competitive tenacity in a sport in which size and speed are dominant. Small by NFL standards, he nonetheless led the Vikings to the Super Bowl three times. Though told he was not big enough to play college ball, let alone professional football, he became one of the all-time greats. Wikipedia acknowledges his accomplishments:

In his 18 NFL seasons, Tarkenton completed 3,686 of 6,467 passes for 47,003 yards and 342 touchdowns, with 266 interceptions. Tarkenton's 47,003 career passing yards rank him 8th all time, while his 342 career passing touchdowns is 6th all-time in NFL history. He also is 6th on the all-time list of wins by a starting quarterback with 124 regular season victories. He also used his impressive scrambling ability to rack up 3,674 rushing yards and 32 touchdowns on 675 carries. During his career, Tarkenton ran for a touchdown in 15 different seasons, an NFL record among quarterbacks. He ranks fourth in career rushing yards among quarterbacks, behind Randall Cunningham, Steve Young, and Michael Vick. He is also one of two NFL quarterbacks ever to rush for at least 300 yards in seven different seasons; the other is Tobin Rote. He was inducted into the Pro Football Hall of Fame in 1986. Vikings head coach Bud Grant flatly called Tarkenton, "the greatest quarterback who's ever played." When he retired, Tarkenton held NFL career records in pass attempts, completions, yardage, touchdowns, rushing yards by a quarterback, and wins by a starting quarterback.

Tarkenton once said, "Fear causes people to draw back from situations. It brings on mediocrity. It dulls creativity. It sets one up to be a loser in life."

I can't imagine what must have gone through his mind the first time he took an NFL snap. There he was, trying to see over a center who was nearly taller, humped over, than Tarkenton was standing, only to see a 6-foot, 5-inch, 260-pound linebacker who could bench press three Fran Tarkenton's, charging right at him. Courage is not the absence of fear; it's the discipline to do what's right in spite of our fear.

John Wayne (For you young guys, John Wayne was the last great cowboy…in motion pictures!) put it this way: "Courage is being scared to death—but saddling up anyway."

We must also understand that fear is not sinful, and it is not necessarily bad. Fear is much like anger in that sense. It's an emotion that can be very healthy when surrendered to God's will. If fear were inherently bad, we wouldn't read in the Bible that the beginning of wisdom is the fear of God. Mighty Men get that.

The positive side of fear

Most parents instill fear of mom and dad into their children at an early age. Fear of repercussions with parents will keep a small child from running out into the street, even though he may not comprehend the danger of being run over. Fear of getting in trouble with mom and dad will keep children from playing with fire, wandering off alone, or climbing up on the roof.

Fear keeps people from doing insane things. It's one (and the best) of many reasons I've never jumped off a 200-foot-high platform tied to a bungee cord, nor jumped out of a perfectly good airplane. I realize that some courageous men will disagree, but I think bungee jumping or parachuting from a plane is downright crazy.

Fear prevents us from doing a lot of things that could be dangerous. It's an innate sense that God gives us for our well-being. When properly understood, fear is our friend. However, when fear is allowed to rule our lives, it becomes tyrannical. When not surrendered to the Lordship of Christ, fear, like anger, can be very destructive.

Webster's Unabridged Dictionary defines fear this way: "A painful emotion or passion excited by an expectation of evil, or the apprehension of impending danger." Scripture explains this fear and its divine design in the Old and New Testaments.

The definition of fear.

Simply defined, fear means, "reverential awe." It's the sensation we all feel in the presence of anything or anyone that overwhelms us. It comes when we stand at the edge of the Grand Canyon and suddenly realize its vastness and our smallness. This sense of awe comes when we look up on a clear night and gaze at the infinite majesty of the Milky Way. The stars and planets testify how great the God is who created the heavens. Scripture defines fear as the awesome reverence that we should know in our spirit when we understand the greatness of God. In fact, the word "fear" can be translated as "wonderful" or "stupendous." When the Bible speaks of beholding our God in fear, it refers to that "reverential awe."

God's design for fear.

God seeks to motivate men to seek His face and do His will. The Bible says, "The fear of the Lord is the beginning of wisdom" (Proverbs 9:10). There is further understanding when we read what it says of Noah in Hebrews 11:7: "By faith Noah, when warned of things not yet seen, in holy fear built an ark to save his family."

What motivated Noah to work for 120 years on a boat so big it would hold two of every animal on the face of the earth? His drive was his family of seven, plus himself and enough food for all. What in the world would possess a man to go through the ridicule and scorn of a world that despised him for the God he loved? The Bible says it was holy fear that moved Noah.

Now think about the world in which he lived. It was a world that totally rejected God. It was a world that laughed him to scorn. It was godless people that called him a fool when he worked every day for

120 straight years. These were individuals who were totally devoted to doing evil. And it was a very violent place. Noah continued because God had spoken to him. He had heard the Word of God, and he feared God more than man. Our Lord designed fear to mobilize us to seek His face and to do His will.

Satan also has a plan for fear. He wants to paralyze man with terror and dread. Studies have shown that 60% of our fears are imaginary and never materialize. Of the remaining 40%, most concern things beyond our control. Only about 5% of that which terrifies us has any real substance. The reality is that when it comes to fear, we can do only three things.

We can avoid any association with anything that causes fear.

For instance, if we have a fear of heights, we may skip riding on a ferris wheel or go near anything that's high. Claustrophobia may mean we avoid elevators. Some men are terrorized by their phobias. Famed aviator and inventor Howard Hughes, who had a morbid fear of disease, tried to live in complete isolation.

We can hope it will go away.

This approach is counterproductive. Rather than solving the problem, this method allows the fear to fester and often makes it worse.

Patton faced his fears.

Men, no one is exempt from fear. We look at a man like George S. Patton and say, "What a courageous man." Army General Patton was hated by many of his fellow World War II officers, because he often put himself and his soldiers at risk. While most of his rank stayed safely out of harm's way, he led his tanks into battle, often riding in a jeep before his men. Patton had a sense of invincibility and defied the odds. His men said he was fearless.

However, the general said of himself, "I am not a brave man. The truth of the matter is I am truly a coward at heart. I have never been near the sound of a shot or the site of a battle in my whole life that I was not afraid. I constantly sweat in my palms and get a lump in my throat. The time to take counsel of your fears is before you make an important battle decision. That's the time to listen to every fear you can imagine. When you've collected all the facts and fear and made your decision, turn off all your fears and go ahead." Mighty Men are like that!

Remember: Courage is not the absence of fear, but rather the discipline to do what's right in spite of your fears. No man is exempt from fear. That's why we must remind ourselves that Satan will use fear to terrorize, neutralize and immobilize us. Faith enables a man to march through fear and do what is needed because it is right. When a person does that, others will say, "What courage!" Mighty Men are like that.

Faith produces miracles

Satan's plan is to paralyze us with terror and dread. Fear can be a good thing, but it can also be destructive. We live in a culture where many people clamor to see God do a miracle to prove His existence. Ours is a culture of increasing cynicism and skepticism. Some in the church have tried to prove God's existence by performing signs and wonders. I recall listening to a talk by one of my favorite teachers, Dr. Chuck Swindoll, renowned author and pastor, and former president of Dallas Theological Seminary. He was teaching on the miracle of healing, focusing on God's ability to cure any disease. After all, He is God! Swindoll then turned to what he called, "miracle mongers."

He began talking about so-called "faith healers," and asked a penetrating question: "Why in the world don't these folks go to hospitals quietly and do the work of Jesus emptying hospital beds if, in fact, they have this miraculous gift of healing? Why do they make it a side show and attract thousands and always appear to be there for the money?" It's important to remember that God does the work of healing, not the man who talks about it.

Can God heal? Oh, yes! Do I believe our God is a God of miracles? Yes! I have witnessed miracles, but I will say this—miracles seldom produce faith. Those who crucified Jesus saw plenty of miracles, but the miracles failed to produce faith. Faith creates miracles, and a man who walks by faith will see the miraculous hand of God. A church that operates by faith will have a miracle story to tell. But, when we focus on the miracles instead of the person of Jesus, we soon find ourselves wanting.

Five loaves became twelve baskets

To understand the negative side of fear, let's examine an event in Jesus' life where he fed a multitude of people and afterward taught a disciple a lesson he would not forget:

> "He directed the people to sit down in the grass, taking the five loaves and the two fish and looking up to heaven, He gave thanks and broke the loaves. Then He gave them to the disciples, and the disciples gave them to the people. They all ate and were satisfied, and the disciples picked up twelve baskets full of broken pieces that were left over. The number of those who ate was about five thousand men, besides women and children.
>
> Immediately Jesus made the disciples get into the boat and go on ahead of Him to the other side, while He dismissed the crowd. After He had dismissed them, He went up on a mountainside by Himself to pray. When the evening came, He was there all alone, but the boat was already a considerable distance from the land, buffeted by waves because the wind was against it.
>
> During the fourth watch of the night, Jesus went out

walking to them, walking on the lake. When the disciples saw Him walking on the lake, they were terrified. 'It's a ghost,' they said and cried out with fear.

But Jesus immediately said to them: 'Take courage! It is I. Don't be afraid.'

'Lord if it's You,' Peter replied, 'tell me to come to You on the water.'

'Come,' He said. Then Peter got down out of the boat, walked on the water and came toward Jesus.

But when he saw the wind, he was afraid and, beginning to sink, cried out, 'Lord, save me!'

Immediately, Jesus reached out His hand and caught him. 'You of little faith,' He said, 'why did you doubt?' And when they climbed into the boat the wind died down.

Then those who were in the boat worshiped Him, saying, 'Truly You are the Son of God.' When they crossed over, they landed in Gennesaret. And when the men of that place recognized Jesus they sent word to all the surrounding country" (Matthew 14:18-35).

Jesus fed 5,000 men, not to mention their wives and their children, with two loaves of bread and two fish. And, when they gathered the fragments, they gathered 12 full baskets. Then all 12 disciples were instructed to get in a boat with the 12 baskets of fragments. Isn't that interesting? A basket apiece. Then, Jesus sent them on their way, and He went to the mountain to pray.

Jesus had just performed a dramatic and dynamic miracle. He fed perhaps as many as 20,000 people (5,000 men and their families) from just a handful of loaves and fish. Can God do that? Yes, He can. However, the mission of Jesus was not to feed the hungry or to perform great miracles. At no point does the Bible say He healed all the sick. We know that He healed only some of the sick. We know that He didn't feed all of the starving people; He fed some of the starving. Some of the sick that He healed, later died of other diseases, and the starving people that He fed got hungry again. His mission was never to just meet physical needs, but to do the will of the Father. Therefore, when He sent the disciples into the boat, He went to the hillside to spend time alone with God. His mission and His passion, was to do the will of His Father.

That sinking feeling

By the time He had finished praying, a storm had engulfed the disciples. Many of these men were seasoned fishermen, yet they were frightened out of their minds. They were so full of fear that when they saw Jesus walking on the water, they thought he was a ghost. Many men become neutralized and unwilling to try anything bold and innovative because they are overwhelmed with fears, many of which are imagined. According to the study, I quoted earlier, only a small percentage of our fears are justifiable. The rest are cooked up in the darkroom of our imaginations, where negatives are developed.

The minds of the disciples saw a ghost because their imaginations were running wild. In the midst of all of this, Jesus said, "Be of good cheer. It is I. Be not afraid." Christ gave them two commands and one statement of fact. If you desire to become a Mighty Man, you have to embrace the one fact that Jesus stated to His men in the boat during that fierce storm: "It is I!" Once you understand the character of God, who cannot lie, and embrace the truth that Jesus will never allow His Mighty Men to enter a storm alone, you will never again envision ghosts, but instead, you will "be of good cheer" and "be not afraid."

The moment Jesus spoke, the men's hearts began to calm down. The actual storm did not subside. It was still raging; the boat was still rocking; the rain was still pelting. But then they heard a familiar voice which said, **"It is I!"** suddenly, with rapt attention, all eyes focused on Jesus, who, just moments before, they imagined to be a ghost. If we are willing to face our fears, often the thing that we fear most will enable us to see Jesus the clearest. Before, they saw a ghost, because they were looking for a ghost.

At the sound of Jesus' voice, Peter said, "If it's really you, tell me to walk on the water." As a man, I admire Peter. He is the only disciple on record to walk on water. Jesus said, "Come," and he got out of the boat and began walking. Let's not forget the kind of day they experienced. In a matter of just a few hours, Peter had witnessed Jesus feeding thousands of men, women, and children with a handful of loaves. They retrieved twelve baskets full of the bread and fish fragments and watched Jesus walking across the water in the midst of the storm. These are things you don't usually see. And now Peter is walking on the water. Mighty Men do that.

Then all of a sudden, he takes his eyes off Jesus, sees the waves, hears the crash of the ocean storm and feels the spray of the water, and he begins to sink.

Overcoming the power of the senses

All of Peter's senses were shouting at him, "You fool! You can't walk on water!" Within moments, he moved from faith to fear as he listened to his five senses instead of trusting in Jesus.

- Hearing. He heard the wind.
- Taste. He tasted the salt water.
- Smell. He smelled the sea.
- Feeling. He felt the ocean spray.
- Sight. He saw the waves and the effects of the storm.

Everything that made him human was shouting: "You can't do this!" and he began to sink. Why? The answer that most people give is that He took his eyes off Jesus.

This may surprise you, but taking his eyes off Jesus was NOT the reason Peter began to sink. It's much deeper than that. In fact, if that's all we take away from this passage, we are likely to sink into our own sea of fears and phobias. Peter saw the miraculous works of Jesus almost daily for three years. Here was a man whose shadow raised people off their deathbeds, as recorded in the book of Acts during that special dispensation of the early church.

So then, what is the real reason Peter began to sink? It's the same reason we sink—he forgot the "Word" of the Lord. He forgot that Jesus had said, "Be of good cheer. Be not afraid. It is I." The only solution for our fears and the only hope we have to overcome them is the Word of our Everlasting and Eternal Lord. "The grass withers and the flowers fall, but the word of our God endures forever" (Isaiah 40:1). Peter later wrote in his first epistle: "All flesh is like grass, and all its glory like the flowers of the field; the grass withers and the flowers fall, but the word of the Lord stands forever" (1 Peter 1:24-25). It is these very Truths to which we are to "take every thought captive and make them obedient" (2 Corinthians 10:5).

Miracles come and go, but it is the Word of God that will remain forever. If we are to stand in this evil day, we must anchor our lives in the infallible and eternal Word of God. Jesus said: "Heaven and earth shall pass away, but My Words shall not pass away" (Matthew 24:35).

John 5:16-30 contains the central theme of our Savior's existence. Jesus said, "What I see the Father doing that I do and what I hear the Father saying, that I say." Our only hope for deliverance from fear is the Word of God. It is the only thing that never changes because Jesus never changes. Scripture assures us that, "Jesus is the same yesterday, today, and forever" (Hebrews 13:8). Mighty Men embrace that truth.

Peter forgot the word of the Lord and listened to his common sense say: "You can't do this!" At that moment he forgot that Jesus had spoken: "It is I. Don't be afraid." He forgot those words and began to sink in fear. We are never going to be able to exempt ourselves entirely from the tyranny of our senses as long as we live in this world, but we must not allow our fears to control us.

There are times in my life, often when I least expect it, that something triggers my fears, and they begin to whisper, "Man, you're in big trouble." I have awakened in the middle of the night in a cold sweat, overwhelmed with a sense of impending doom. But then I remember the Word of the Lord, and fear departs. That's my anchor, and it has been for six decades. I am also reminded of the promise in 2 Chronicles 16:9, "The eyes of the Lord range throughout the earth, seeking to strengthen those whose hearts are committed to Him." At the moment we choose to believe His Word rather than give into fear, His gaze stops on us and strengthens our hearts.

If we anchor our lives on anything other than the Word of God; if we attach ourselves to any personality other than Jesus, we are destined for failure. If we don't keep our focus on Jesus, sooner or later, our senses will win out; we'll follow our emotions and sink.

We were born with five senses, and we will die with them. However, God's Word says, "I am crucified with Christ, nevertheless I live, yet not I, but the life that I now live, I live by faith in the Son of God Who loves me and gave Himself for me" (Galatians 2:20). This passage refers to our flesh being crucified with Christ so that we no longer have to obey its demands. The crucified life enables men to walk in a discipline of daily death to self so that we don't allow the flesh to drive us from one emotional moment to the next. It is the ultimate in real liberty. In a spirit of discipline, Mighty Men focus on the Word and do what God says, even when it doesn't feel right. Peter began to sink, not because of the wind or the waves, but because he forgot the Word.

Jesus also says, "Be of good cheer." Peter believed by faith that if Jesus was with him, and told him to be of good cheer, he could trust Him. In fact, initially, Peter felt so much happiness that he said to himself, "I'll just get out of this boat and walk with Jesus."

Many individuals are drowning in their circumstance right now because they've forgotten how faithful God is. In the eye of the storm, we believe what we can see. We believe what we can hear.

We believe what we can smell. We believe what we can taste. And, we believe what we can feel. Our emotions tell us that disaster is pending. But when we learn to live by faith in God's Word, we can rise above all of that. Mighty Men live by faith, not by sight.

Ever present, but conquerable

Now, some may wonder if the fear ever leaves. George S. Patton said he never faced a battle where his hands didn't sweat; inside of him, everything he had was quivering. But he isolated himself from his emotions. He had decided what he would do in advance, and he stuck to the plan. He figured the troops needed to see him drive out in front of the tank brigade, so no matter how he felt, and no matter how hot the battle, that is what he did.

We live in a generation today where senses drive people. But here's the good news: Peter's Savior overcame—and still does. On his way down, Peter said, "Lord, help me." There is not a real father alive who, upon hearing his child cry out, "Help me," would not try to help. And, our God who loves us infinitely, more than we love our children, is not going to ignore our cries for help either. Matthew 7:11 (NKJV) says, "If you then, being evil, know how to give good gifts to your children, how much more will your Father who is in heaven give good things to those who ask Him!" The smartest thing we will ever say when we're drowning in our fears is, "Lord, help me!" Mighty Men do that!

How do you think Peter got back to the boat? Either he walked hand in hand with the Lord, or the Lord carried him. Either way is a great way to travel!

Jesus said to His disciples, "You of little faith.... why did you doubt?" Paul the Apostle said; "Faith cometh by hearing and hearing by the word of God" (Romans 10:17). The more of God's Word we place in our hearts and minds, the stronger our faith will be. And, the stronger our faith, the more disciplined our fear, such that it will not immobilize us but enable us to live in victory.

Mighty Men Overcome Fear

We must overcome fear if we are ever going to be Mighty Men. In order to overcome fear, we must first remember that fear is not always bad. Secondly, we must recognize that uncontrolled fear will destroy us. And, finally, we must remember that courage is not the absence of fear, but rather the discipline to do what's right, in spite of our fear.

Dear friend, let me remind you that Peter didn't start sinking because he took his eyes off Jesus. He could have looked anywhere he wanted had he stayed in good cheer, believing the words of Jesus when He said, "It is I, don't be afraid." He could have said, "Man, look at the size of that wave! This is so cool! Just me and you, Lord, huh?" Peter began to sink when he forgot the Word of the Lord. Mighty Men can sink, too!

Have you forgotten the Word of the Lord? Men have yet to invent a problem or face a challenge that is not addressed either directly or in principle in God's Word. There is no greater guidebook for our lives than the Bible. We can overcome our fears in direct proportion to the amount of God's Word we embrace. We must seek Him. We must spend time with Him. We must desire to know Him intimately and then live like it, even in the face of fear. Mighty Men do!

Chapter Eleven

HOW TO MANAGE TIME

"The 4x100-Meter Relay"

The wisdom of Solomon says, "There It's a time for everything, and a season for every activity under heaven. . . ." (Ecc. 3:1).

Time is our most precious commodity and a priceless possession. One spent second can never be repeated or recouped, making time management a priority for everyone seeking to make the most of his time on earth. How do we manage our time? A real life appropriately balances worship, work, family and personal wellbeing. The 4x100-meter relay offers some parallels that will help us win our race to become a Mighty Man.

The 4x100 has potential for exhilarating achievement or great disappointment. It's all about time management, combined with speed. The 4x100-meter relay starts with the explosion of the starter's gun and finishes less than 40 seconds later, with the four winning runners celebrating.

At the outset, the first runner explodes out of the blocks with the baton and races to the 100-meter mark. If he leaves the blocks early, the gun fires a second time to indicate a false start, and the race must start over. If he makes a second false start, his team is disqualified. The lead runner hands off the baton to the next, and so on until four sprinters have covered 100 meters each, managing successful exchanges along the way. In a matter of seconds, all of their training and efforts are either rewarded with victory or disappointment.

Each teammate receives the baton within a 20-meter area. Any pass before or after that area is illegal, and will result in the disqualification of the team, making managing the exchange as important as speed. If a runner drops the baton while passing or in the middle of the race, the team is disqualified. If a runner waiting for the baton takes off a split second too soon, the runner exchanging the baton can be forced to run beyond the allotted space. Likewise, if the runner awaiting the baton waits a split second too long, the runner passing the baton will have to break stride rather than risk running past the waiting runner. This error in timing exponentially increases the potential for bungling the exchange.

The 4x100-meter relay is a picture of time management like no other event. Everything happens so quickly. Each person must do his part to perfection. Every runner on the four-man team is critical for victory.

The sum total of life

While not as regimented as a relay race, our lives are lived in time segments. Every hour is 60 minutes; every day is 24 hours; every week is seven days; every month has an allotted time, and every year is 12 months. According to Scripture, three score and ten (70 years) comprise a typical life. When we look back over our lives thus far, we should ask, "What is the sum total of my life?"

Steven Covey's two books, *Seven Habits of Highly Successful People*, and the sequel, *First Things First*; Dr. Kenneth Blanchard's and Dr. Spencer Johnson's book, *The One-Minute Manager*, and *Ordering Your Private World* by Gordon MacDonald, have all been very helpful to me, and I recommend them highly. All four books provide practical suggestions for time management that can aid us in becoming Mighty Men.

Life is composed of a series of events. How we choose to spend our time, determines our level of personal and professional success in life. In an age with so many demands on us, learning how to manage time becomes paramount. Time management is of particular importance for Christians, who know they will someday be held accountable for their lives before God.

In *First Things First*, Steven Covey titled the first chapter: "No One Ever Despairs on His Deathbed of Not Having Spent More Time at The Office." He reminds us that no man at the end laments not playing "one more round of golf." No man on his deathbed regrets many of the things that so often consume our time. In the greater scheme of life, most things are not all that important.

It's apparent that some people live for tomorrow, while some live for yesterday. But we want to live life to the fullest every day. The following are some noteworthy facts:

Fact #1: Our days on earth are pre-determined.

Ecclesiastes 3:2 reveals that there is a time appointed unto man to be born, and a time for him to die. Ultimately, we have no more control over when we will die than when we were born. Some say that scientific advances will change this. Perhaps so, but even if man gains the ability to clone another human being and every state enacts legislation allowing doctors assisted suicide (and both certainly looks like a possibility), God will not relinquish His role as the Author of life, and He will still hold man accountable for his life on earth. Scripture warns us: "It is appointed unto man once to die and after that the judgment" (Hebrews 9:27).

We are going to answer to God, and man cannot change that equation. He may ignore God, and he may refuse to recognize God as his creator. Scripture, however, is clear that there will come a time when every knee will bow, and every tongue will confess that Jesus Christ is Lord (Romans 14:11). Further, the Bible clearly states that there is a time for everything, including a time to be born and a time to die. Moreover, no man knows when his hour will come. (Matthew 25:13) We may think we are aware of a lot of things, but apart from the sin of suicide, we don't know when our hour will come.

I had a friend who prided himself on keeping physically and intellectually fit. But at the age of 30, his doctor diagnosed him with a brain tumor and told the family that he would probably die within six months. That's when all of us who knew and loved him began to pray.

Doctors' predictions of time frames are educated guesses at best. My friend lived another five years, after receiving that first grim diagnosis. While his doctors were amazed, his wife and three children were grateful for each additional day God had given them with their beloved husband and father.

As a pastor, I have presided over funerals for several people who died quite young. Inevitably in those cases, someone laments that the individual's life was cut short. When we buried our youngest child, Kathryn, at the tender age of 25, many said this of her. Who are we mere mortals to think or say such things? The Lord of life determines a lifespan, and He alone knows how long life should be. It's the quality of your life, not how long you breathe, that matters. (In the appendix of this book are two poems I wrote just after Kathryn went to Heaven. One of the poems deals with this sensitive subject.)

Fact #2: No one is assured of any time beyond the present.

Jesus said in Matthew 6:27, "Who of you by worrying can add a single hour to his life?" We can try to extend our lives by making sure we eat right, exercise faithfully, taking vitamins and herbs and doing everything the experts tell us to do. But try as we might, we cannot add a single day to our lives. He may will you to begin doing all those things so you can live a fuller and better life, but He alone extends a life!

Someone wrote a verse that provides a proper perspective on each day:

"Yesterday is history.

Tomorrow is a mystery.

Today is a gift.

That's why we call it the present."

We should live and receive each day as the precious gift that it is.

Fact #3: Everyone gets the same amount of time each day.

I've learned, if I want to get something done, to look for someone who is busy and ask them to do it. Most often, if someone is not busy, there's a reason. One of the most difficult tasks your pastor faces is finding someone who is not already overloaded who will take a job and do it. The dependable are busy, and the undependable are…undependable. Which characterizes you?

All of us have accepted tasks that we haven't finished, or handled with less care than we should have. But those should be the exceptions in our lives, rather than the rule. Ask yourself, "Am I responsibly finishing projects I start? Am I doing what I said I would do?" I'm amazed, and at times humbled, by how much some people get done and how little others do in the same 24 hours.

Are we known as someone who can be trusted to start and finish a job? Everyone wakes up in the morning with the same amount of allotted time. Tomorrow starts at 12:00 midnight, tonight. God doesn't look down from Heaven and turn to the angels and say; "There are about 15 people who haven't finished yesterday, so let's just delay tomorrow by an hour." Life doesn't work like that. We each have 24 hours in the day, yet some get far more done than others. That's because they manage their time better. What we do with each day becomes the measure of our life.

In Steven Covey's book *First Things First*, he discusses what he calls Quadrants of Time. I'm going to borrow his idea and call them

Category 1, Category 2, Category 3, and Category 4.

A one-day clock could be divided into the following four categories:

Category one Necessity	Category two Values
Category Three Discernment	Category Four Defeat

Everyone is allotted the same quantity of time each day. When our obituaries are written, what will be said about how we used our time on earth?

Category One: (Necessity) is driven by demand.

These are things over which we have no control, things that must be done to live. For instance, if we want to live responsibly, we have to work. Our career choice determines the amount of time required. For example, obstetricians have fewer choices regarding how they schedule their time than a writer or an artist. When a patient goes into labor, the obstetrician doesn't have the luxury of saying, "I'll run to the hospital when I finish my golf game." Those who are married to someone in such a profession are also forced to make concessions when their spouses drop everything and respond to emergencies.

Every career parallels the career of the obstetrician to one degree or another. There is a portion of everyone's life in which there are few options. This is the "No Choice" category. We must commit a certain amount of our time, if we are to succeed in our chosen profession.

There are other ways in which this category of time is not option-filled. You must allocate six to eight hours for sleep every night. If you refuse to do so, there are enormous consequences to your health. You cannot ignore some things. Mighty Men understand this and allocate their time accordingly.

Category Two: (Value) is driven by design.

To be truly successful in life, a person must establish certain non-negotiable priorities. These priorities are different from Category One for this reason. While some things in Category Two are very important, they are also voluntary. You make time for such priorities because you value them, but they can be set aside if necessary for more pressing matters. For instance, you may value daily exercise but skip it occasionally if something more important arises.

Another personal priority that would fall under this category would be our daily quiet time with the Lord. We know we need to spend this time with God and value it, but because no one is forcing us to do so, we may occasionally push it aside.

Because you value time alone with God, you seldom choose to skip it. Time off from work also falls into this category. We know we need some time away, and value time with the family away from work. However, when some great project comes up, we may choose to delay our vacation and go to the office instead. Mighty Men prioritize their lives.

Category Three: (Discernment) is driven by need.

Many things appear to be urgent, but we need discernment to determine if they require our immediate attention. Several years ago, I was listening to the tape of Gordon MacDonald's well-known book, *Ordering Your Private World*. He noted that early in his ministry, every time he heard the telephone ring and the caller had an "urgent" need, he felt compelled to drop everything he was doing and respond to the individual immediately. One Saturday afternoon a lady called him and said, "Pastor, I have to see you right now!"

He could tell by the tone of her voice that things were terrible. He tried to calm her down and diagnose the level of crisis. He learned that her urgent problem was that her husband had left her.

This was a serious matter. However, as they spoke, he found out that her husband had been gone for a while and that there had been a growing chasm in their relationship for years.

Never before had she considered it an emergency, but suddenly it was an urgent matter that demanded her pastor's immediate response. Pastor MacDonald agreed to meet her but felt that meeting with her alone at the church on a Saturday night was unwise. She agreed.

He also shared with her that Saturday was his one night to spend with his family and for final preparation of the next morning's Sunday message, which would reach thousands who attended his church. He reminded her that this was where they had initially become connected, and his preaching had impacted her life in a positive way. She agreed. He suggested that she call the office early Monday morning and schedule an appointment with his secretary.

This answer would keep him from breaking several commitments he had made to his family and himself. The lady hung up, thankful for a pastor who had his priorities straight. They met the following week, and he was able to help her. It required discernment for Pastor McDonald to determine where her crisis ranked in importance in his schedule.

There are moments in each of our lives when something urgent intrudes into our carefully planned schedule, and we must discern whether to stop everything and focus solely on it. Though it may seem critical from one perspective, we need to learn to recognize the differences between:

1. Things that are urgent and demand immediate attention;
2. Things that are important but not urgent; and…
3. Things that seem urgent until weighed in light of God's overall plan for our lives.

Dealing with fear falls under this category as well. There are times when a sense of dread comes crashing upon us, and we're overwhelmed with the feeling that something is very wrong. If we're not careful, we'll panic and drop everything we had planned to do, to deal with the fear that we may later discover was more imagined than real. The discerning heart considers this truth: "God does not give us a spirit of fear, but of power, of love and a sound mind" (2 Timothy 1:7). Many of those things we fear most never come to pass. It takes discernment and a sound mind to determine if the fear we feel is real or imagined. Mighty Men develop keen discernment.

Category Four: (Defeat) is driven by waste.

We must work to avoid wasting time. For instance, watching television without discretion can waste more hours than most of us want to admit. You can sit down to look at the evening news and mid-way through you see a promotion for a program that will follow. It sounds, and seems, so appealing that you decide you deserve a little entertainment. Before long, you look up and realize you've wasted several hours and have nothing to show for it.

By the way, you need to plan for such times occasionally, because everyone needs time to relax. But there is a difference between planning to relax and being victimized by wasted time, stolen because you weren't vigilant. This same dynamic works with Facebook, Twitter, and other potential time-wasters.

When Category Four becomes the dominate quadrant of our time usage, we're on the trail to a life of despair, defeat and discouragement. Take a close look again at the diagrams. In Category One there is no choice. However, there are many choices in Categories Two, Three, and Four. The wise person makes smart decisions as he allocates his time each day. The wise man will stop everything else and say, "My wife needs time with me, and all this other stuff can wait." Or he'll say, "My children need time with me, so I'll move some appointments and make time for them." Or, "My friend is hurting and needs my time right now."

An overloaded schedule feeds a false sense of self-worth, and soon becomes a tyrant that's never satisfied, demanding more and more of our time. There is something ego-inflating in being able to say, "I've got a flight to catch," or "I've got a meeting I must attend." Are you really needed or are you just massaging your self-esteem by accepting so many requests? The same can be said of an appointment log or calendar of events. Are you serving yourself, or are you serving God and others, with the limited time you have on this earth?

We need to ask ourselves these three essential questions:

1. In the greater scheme of God's plan for my life, am I using my time to build His kingdom or my resume?

2. How much of what I do today will make any difference 10,000 years from now?

3. Is there something I could be doing right now that I'm not doing, that would enhance me professionally or personally if I began doing it today?

Ultimately, when we stand before God, He will not care whether or not we filled each page of our calendar. His concern will be whether or not we fulfilled His divine plan for our lives. Did we pay attention to the important things in life? Three categories of our time, out of four, involve choices we have to make. The choices that we make reflect our values. Mighty Men understand that!

Making a tough choice

In the 1996 Olympic Games, the U.S. track team was embroiled in a swirling controversy. By Olympic standards, 35-year-old Carl Lewis was considered a bit of a risk against younger sprinters, despite his continuing success. Had he been allowed to run one of the four legs of the 4x100-meter relay for Team USA, he would have been competing for his 10th Olympic gold medal. However, the coaches decided that others who qualified deserved their chance to win a medal and passed over Lewis. The U.S. team had dominated the event for more than 80 years, and no one even considered they might fail to win the gold.

The leadoff man, Jon Drummond, gave the U.S. a slight lead. But, the final three sprinters were beaten by their Canadian counterparts, who took the gold. The Americans settled for silver. There has been much speculation about whether Carl Lewis would have changed the results had he run. Would he have had a calming effect on the team with his vast experience? Would he have caught the Canadian with his blazing speed running the last leg? My point in raising this issue is that the decision to replace Lewis was a choice.

We have choices to make every single day, and the summation of our choices determines whether we will be a success in life or a failure.

We've looked at three facts about time so far.

Fact #1: Our days on this earth have already been predetermined.
Fact #2: No one is assured any time beyond the present. And...
Fact #3: Everyone is allotted the same amount of time each day.

Finally, we come to the last, but not least, point.

Fact #4: Time is precious.

The writer of Hebrews says in 9:27, "... man is destined to die once, and after that to face judgment."

My first full-time position in ministry was with evangelist Mickey Bonner when I was only 20. I transferred to Houston Baptist University for my senior year to finish my undergraduate degree and prepare for seminary. He allowed me to travel across the nation and take young people out into the streets and show them how to win souls for Christ.

What a year that was. I enjoyed the opportunity of traveling while going back and forth to Houston to take classes. I had the privilege of seeing hundreds of young people give their hearts to Christ.

At the end of the year, I resigned and began preparing to enroll in Southwestern Baptist Theological Seminary in Fort Worth, to begin my formal theological training for ministry. Over the ensuing years, Mickey and I remained good friends, though we didn't get to see each other much. Our ministries took us to opposite corners of the world.

One day, over twenty years later, I was out promoting my first book, *Enough is Enough*. I looked up, and there was Mickey Bonner. We had a great visit, and he gave me an autographed copy of his new book, *Brokenness*. The next couple of months after that encounter I was privileged to run into him several more times, for which I am very grateful.

One Thursday night, after preaching in a church, he stepped out of the pulpit and dropped dead. He died just like he wanted—preaching the Gospel of Jesus Christ. When I heard the news of his death, God said to my heart, "My son, time is precious." I had no idea when we bumped into each other just a few short weeks earlier that I was seeing him for the last time. We never know when we peer into the eyes of another fellow human being if we are seeing him for the last time or not. Time is precious.

Believe me, when God chose to call Kathryn home on October 27, 2004, I came to realize how short, unpredictable, and fleeting is our time on this earth. My wife and I had no idea that when Kathryn went to sleep on October 26, she would awaken the next morning in Heaven. Time is so very precious.

Finally, we need to realize that time will someday be suspended. Time is linear in this era. Theologically we call this era a "dispensation." It's time in which God works in a certain way. I looked in the Greek concordance and discovered several Greek words which all translated into the same English word: time.

One spoke to a particular point in time. Another word is used to describe a period of time like an hour. Still another word is used to describe a fixed segment of time. The Scriptures use all three words. The Greek language, unlike our English language, is very precise.

This world and the next

There will come a time, in our lives, when time, as we now know it, will be suspended. The Bible says, "But do not forget this one thing, dear friends: With the Lord, a day is like a thousand years, and a thousand years are like a day" (2 Peter 3:8). Our eternal, omnipotent, omniscient and omnipresent God is not confined to time or space as we are.

After His crucifixion and resurrection, Jesus could walk right through walls. He could also transcend time and be here one moment and somewhere else the next. After we get through with this linear world in which we express time in seconds, hours, and days, we will come to a period that the Bible calls eternity, when God suspends all time. Depending on what we do during our allotted time here on earth, we will either live forever in a place of eternal blessing or eternal torment, Heaven or Hell. Time is precious.

We are alive today so that we can make sure we are right with God. The moment that we breathe our last breath in this world we will find ourselves in an eternal world. The Bible says that if we die without a relationship with God through Christ, we will live forever in torment. Revelation 20:10 speaks of when God casts Satan into the Lake of Fire, where forever he will live in torment. In the same manner, everyone who has rejected Christ will find himself catapulted into a timeless place of torment called Hell. The person who has become presumptuous of time, and puts off a relationship with Christ, will find his fate to be the same as the great deceiver, Satan. "It is appointed unto man once to die, and after that, the judgment" (Hebrews 9:27). It's vital that those of us who know Jesus as our Savior to be "prepared to give an answer to everyone who asks you to give the reason for the hope that you have" (1 Peter 3:15).

If you can't point to a given moment in your life when you gave your life to Jesus Christ, then you need to do so today.

Time is of the essence. Mighty Men get that.

Chapter Twelve

OVERCOMING THE DEVIL'S "3 D's"

Defeat, Discouragement, and Despair

"The 800-Meter Run"

As I mentioned in an earlier chapter, our ninth-grade football coach basically resorted to blackmail in order to field a track team. He made it clear that if we wanted to receive our football jackets, we had to run track. He assigned me the 440. Others had to run the 880, the mile, the mile relay and so forth, so I got off relatively easy.

The longer runs were brutal!

The 880, now called the 800-meter run, was among the most demanding races, requiring speed and stamina. A friend, whom I'll only call Ed, was among those chosen to run that one. He was about 6' 6" tall and weighed about 180 pounds and he did not like to run long distances. However, because the coach told him this was his event, he trained.

There was one meet in our season that meant more than others. We trained all season for it because we were competing against two other schools in our district and we knew many of the runners we'd be competing against. On the day of the big meet, our coach reminded the long distance runners to pace themselves.

When the gun sounded for the 880, Ed left everyone else in the dust. At the 220 marker, he was 10 to 15 yards in front of the pack. At the first quarter mile, he was a full 20 yards ahead. By now, we were on the edge of our seats cheering and wondering if he could actually win. Ed made it around the next turn, and though he was still doing fine, he was showing signs of fatigue. When he reached the 660 marker, he suddenly slowed down, and apparently exhausted and out of gas, he worked his way over to the side of the track and managed to fall into the long jump sandpit for a relatively safe landing. He timed it just right so that he fell between long jumpers. We were stunned.

Our coach looked at the rest of us after the race and then directly at me and said: "Scarborough, take a couple of guys over there and get Ed's shoes and shirt and leave him in the pit." Poor Ed had been doing so well. But all of a sudden everything changed. It wasn't easy for him to find that pit for his landing, but he apparently thought it would be easier than trying to finish. For the record, we didn't actually leave him there.

I'm often reminded of this story when I find myself counseling or relating to someone experiencing a crisis in their life. Many men are living stressful lives and, at times, the stress becomes too much. No one is immune, and it's easy to find yourself facing defeat, discouragement, and despair, or as I choose to call them, the devil's "3 D's," if you take your eyes off of Jesus. This chapter has been written to provide some tools to deal with such times. Remember that you are never alone and that others have successfully overcome the devil's "3 D's."

We have all encountered men who seemed to be running the race so well when suddenly, they turn and fall into a pit. We're living in a culture where many lose heart and give up. But in doing so, they forfeit the privilege of standing before God someday and hearing Him say: "Well done thou good and faithful servant." Why do so many men exercise their option to quit?

Men today have attained more wealth and material possessions and have more leisure time than any previous generation yet we find more depressed and anxious men than at anytime in our nation's history. Drug abuse is at an all time high, and whether its prescribed medication or illegal drugs that are being consumed, many men are trying to find an escape from their inner turmoil. When you add to that the enormous quantity of alcohol that's daily consumed in our nation, you begin to grasp how pervasive is this problem.

Today's modern man has access to computers, iPads, cell phones, and untold numbers of gadgets designed to make life more efficient and easier, and yet life has become more complex and complicated, resulting in depression and despair for many. We are the most connected generation, with thousands of friends and acquaintances just a click away, and yet there has never been more of a sense of aloneness and hopelessness among many men. Is it any wonder that so many are discouraged to the point of wanting to just quit?

I discovered a book several years ago as I was preparing a message on men going through a "midlife crisis," written by Dr. Harold Kaplan and Dr. Benjamin Sadock. The book was entitled *Synopsis of Psychiatry*, which contained some excellent incite on the subject. They wrote that between 70-80% of men go through a moderate to severe crisis as they enter their 40's and 50's due to several factors. If their findings are correct, then every Mighty Man must be aware of the danger and prepared for confronting such a crisis, in order to successfully negotiate the troubled waters that may await them. "The prudent see danger and take refuge, but the simple keep going and pay the penalty" (Proverbs 22:3). Among the reasons some men face a crisis during their lives are as follows:

1. For some, it's the awareness of mortality.

This knowledge may come as a shocking revelation. The awareness of mortality can be overwhelming. When young, we feel invincible. We know that bad things happen, but not to us.

When we're young, we can compartmentalize life and move on without showing much effect. But men lose that feeling of invincibility as they get older and experience a growing sense of mortality.

2. The discrepancy between ambition and accomplishment.

At some point, all men are forced to revisit their list of life goals and compare them to their achievements. Many cannot handle the immense discrepancy. If men are not careful, financial success and the competence that naturally comes with age can lead to boredom.

This is particularly the case if new challenges and adventures are not forthcoming.

3. Anxiety about what the future will bring.

Even those who have great wealth tend to wonder if it will be there tomorrow. Younger men may find themselves fearful there won't be a good paying job awaiting them as graduation approaches. Older men begin to see their thinning hair changing color or disappearing. This apprehension, whether we are young or old, can bring a sense of panic. We start stumbling, tripping, and compounding the problem. The harder we try to fix it, the greater it becomes. Ultimately, if we keep stumbling, the very thing we fear overtakes us.

Lessons from Elijah

God addressed the devil's 3D's and provided the proper way to deal with them, thousands of years ago, by revealing how one of His most famous prophets dealt with them. While the settings and issues were vastly different from those confronting this present generation, the principles set forth for overcoming the devil's "3D's" are timeless. Let's take a look at Elijah. His story is recounted in full in the book of 1 Kings. He stepped to the center stage during the reign of arguably Israel's most wicked King and Queen, Ahab and Jezebel. "And Elijah the Tishbite, of the inhabitants of Gilead, said to Ahab, 'As the Lord God of Israel lives, before whom I stand, there shall not be dew nor rain these years, except at my word.' And, there was no rain" (1 Kings 17:1). At the time of this exchange, Elijah fearless and respected by all as a true man of God. Then, in 1Kings 19, we find Elijah in the middle of a major crisis.

You and I have a calling on our lives as surely as Elijah. God may not have called you to be a pastor, but God, nevertheless, has called you. Perhaps it is as simple as being a godly father or husband or employee. But we know for certain that He has called each of us to represent Him to the world in which we have been placed. I believe that every man who is married and has a family has a unique calling to be 1) a godly person; 2) a godly spouse, and 3) a godly parent—at a minimum. Just as Elijah did, we must respond to our calling.

Elijah wasn't capable of standing before King Ahab on his own. He was blessed and set apart by God to do a particular job, just as each of us has been to fulfill our calling. God will never call us to do anything we're not equipped to do. Tragically, many men run from their assignments, saying things like, "I just can't live the Christian life. It's too hard." And they're right—in their power they cannot. No one can. However, Christ will enable and grant the strength to any man to accomplish whatever he leads them to do if they place their trust in Him.

Why did God use Elijah so magnificently?

1. Elijah was an available vessel.

He stood before the king and said it was not going to rain. Then he disappeared, and the drought began. It continued for months until everyone was starving—everyone that is, except for Elijah. The Lord blessed him in the quiet solitude of a widow's home. There is always safety and provision for the faithful servant of God.

2. Elijah heard from God because he listened.

When God spoke, the prophet listened. It's of vital importance for men to attend church and listen to what God has laid on their pastor's heart. But, we must not forget that each of us has the same access to God as the preacher, and God will speak to any man who will listen. Hebrews 4:15-16 reminds us, "We do not have a high priest who is unable to sympathize with our weaknesses, but we have one who was tempted in every way that we are, yet was without sin. Let us then approach the throne of grace with confidence, so that we may receive mercy and find grace to help us in our time of need." Mighty Men do that!

3. Elijah was obedient.

God's assignment to Elijah was very dangerous. He told him to march into the king's house and tell Ahab that his great military strength and the acclaim of men meant nothing. It was Elijah's job to announce that the Lord God of heaven was in charge, not King Ahab! Carrying this kind of message to a godless ruler required courage, and it could have cost Elijah his life.

We next find Elijah in a face-off with the false prophets of Baal, on Mount Carmel (1 Kings 18:17-40). The prophets of Baal called upon their god, praying for rain and fire to fall from heaven but to no avail. Then Elijah built an altar of stones. He dug a ditch around it, placed the sacrifice on the top of the wood and called for water to be poured over his sacrifice three times. Elijah then called upon his God, and God sent fire down from heaven, burned the sacrifice, the wood, and the stones and licked up the water in the ditch. God proved He was more powerful than false gods. Next, at God's instruction, Elijah killed all of the false prophets of Baal.

4. Elijah later suffered defeat and grave discouragement.

If we look closely at this series of events in Elijah's life, we find principles that every man of God will need in their life to overcome the devil's "3 D's," when he attacks...and he will attack sooner of later. No one is exempt.

How does a man go from the mountaintop of victory on Mount Carmel, and then plummet to the valley of defeat and discouragement and even thoughts of suicide? We find ourselves asking, "What happened to Elijah?"

"Now Ahab told Jezebel everything Elijah had done and how he had killed all the prophets with the sword. So Jezebel sent a messenger to Elijah to say, 'May the gods deal with me, be it ever so severely if by this time tomorrow I do not make your life like that of one of them.'

Elijah was afraid and ran for his life. When he came to Beersheba in Judah, he left his servant there, while he went a day's journey into the wilderness. He came to a broom bush, sat down under it and prayed that he might die. 'I have had enough, Lord,' he said. 'Take my life; I am no better than my ancestors'" (1 Kings 19:1-4).

How can a man, so greatly used by God, who intimately knew the power of God and the God of power, find himself in a cave despairing of life? It's here that we realize, no one is exempt from discouragement and despair. No one! Depression, despondency, and despair—the devil's "3 D's"—are seeking to destroy every man who follows the path of Elijah. But God reminds us that we are not alone, even when the dark moments come:

"When you pass through the waters, I will be with you; And through the rivers, they will not overflow you. When you walk through the fire, you will not be scorched, nor will the flame burn you.... Do not fear, for I am with you" (Isaiah 43:2,5).

Only two people have been exempt from passing through death on this earth. One was Enoch, of whom the Bible simply says he was no more (see Genesis 5:21-24). The other was Elijah, whom God took up while Elisha the prophet looked on. "As they were walking along and talking together, suddenly a chariot of fire and horses of fire appeared and separated the two of them, and Elijah went up to heaven in a whirlwind" (2 Kings 2:11).

How in the world could Elijah, who knew such exploits, get to a place where he begged God take his life? Men, we're talking suicide, here!

God did not leave us without clues. I love God's Word because He never glosses over a man's weaknesses or failures. God does not shield us from seeing the flaws in our heroes, but rather uses their failures to remind us that anyone can fall. Better yet, God can restore any man that comes to him for help, during such times. Romans 15:4 instructs us, "Everything that was written in the past was written to teach us so that through the endurance taught in the Scriptures and the encouragement they provide we might have hope."

Why did Elijah fall?

1. Elijah forgot.

Elijah is the one who stood on Mount Carmel and prayed down the fire of God upon the soaked and drenched sacrifice. Elijah is the one who stood against 450 prophets of Baal and hundreds besides and said to the people of Israel, "If God be God then serve Him, if Baal be God then serve him," to which they responded in unison, "We will serve God." This same man forgot the divine power that his own eyes had witnessed. He forgot what God could do.

How quickly we all forget. That's why we need to gather in God's house every Sunday, and not just on special occasions or holidays. Hebrews 10:25 (NKJV), exhorts us; "Not forsaking the assembling of ourselves together, as is the manner of some, but exhorting one another, and so much the more as you see the Day approaching." What day? The day of our Lord's return, which is closer now than it has ever been.

As pressures intensify and Satan's hordes unleash their venom on earth, we have to be reminded, through the preaching of God's Word and the encouragement of God's saints, that our God reigns. It's only from another believer that we will hear that message. We won't hear on the nightly news that God reigns. We can read the paper or Internet news sites, but we'll not read that God reigns. We are all prone to forget that God reigns. Mighty Elijah forgot. We can forget too, at our peril.

2. Elijah feared (1 Kings 19:3).

Jezebel, the queen, heard about the altar and how the people were turning back to God. In great anger, she swore to kill Elijah.

But how could he fear her when he had stood before Ahab and said, "I defy you, and I defy those prophets. My God reigns."

Fear fills the vacuum that occurs when faith is depleted. When we're full of faith, fear is dispatched. That doesn't mean fear will not again rise within us. Nor does it mean the devil won't attack our minds, looking for spiritual weakness. However, when an attack comes, Mighty Men can resist it by standing on the Word of God. The Bible says that faith cometh by hearing and hearing by the Word of God (Romans 10:17).

The real battle is fought in the spiritual realm. You must never forget that we wrestle not against flesh and blood, but against principalities and powers and spiritual wickedness in the high places (Ephesians 6:12). Satan's mission is to destroy every one of us. Elijah despaired because of what he forgot and began to fear.

3. Elijah fled.

Like a flood, fear overcame him, and his natural impulse was to flee. Perhaps you have been running from God and allowing Satan to rob you of the victory that God has secured for you. It's never God's will that we cower before fear and run. It may be God's will that we pull back at times. It may be God's will that we remove ourselves from some activity or ministry and rest. But God never intends for his Mighty Men to flee in fear. When we do that, we stumble into darkness which results in greater danger. When we fail to face a situation that is clobbering us spiritually, it never gets better on its own. You must turn to God's Word and stand in faith. Scripture gives us a warning and a solution; "God opposes the proud but gives grace to the humble. So humble yourselves before God. Resist the devil, and he will flee from you. Come close to God, and God will come close to you."

In every trial, we face, God is using it to teach us some eternal truth.

3. Elijah forsook.

Elijah forgot. Elijah feared. Elijah fled. And, as a result, Elijah abandoned thousands of people who had just torn down their idols and burned down the altars dedicated to Baal. He forsook and removed himself from those who believed his message and were celebrating the great victory. All Elijah had left when he ran was one servant, and when he reached his destination, he even sent him away.

There are times when we need to be alone, but not when the "3 D's" are stalking us, leaving us more vulnerable to satanic suggestion. Isolation and withdrawal can lead to self-destruction, as we become susceptible to Satan's harmful suggestions. We forget that "God's thoughts toward us are good, not evil, all the days of our lives" (Jeremiah 29:11). We forget that God has a great plan for our lives (John 10:10). We forget the great victories of the past.

Elijah, as many men do in this state of mind, started pulling away and isolating himself. Before long he found himself saying, "I have failed, I want to die." The greatest fear men have (whether they admit it or not) is the fear of failure. If we withdraw and isolate ourselves, we will begin entertaining destructive thoughts instead of facing our fear in faith.

The first key to facing down the devil's "3 D's" is to admit that you're in a crisis and need God's help. You must recognize that Scripture addresses every crisis you will ever face, and you must be willing to receive God's instruction.

In I Kings 19:11-19, God takes Elijah to the woodshed. Read what God says and what Elijah does in response:

> Then He said, "Go out, and stand on the mountain before the Lord." And behold, the Lord passed by, and a great and strong wind tore into the mountains and broke the rocks in pieces before the Lord, but the Lord was not in the wind; and after the wind an earthquake, but the Lord was not in the earthquake; and after the earthquake a fire, but the Lord was

not in the fire, and after the fire a still small voice.

So it was, when Elijah heard it, that he wrapped his face in his mantle and went out and stood at the entrance of the cave. Suddenly a voice came to him, and said, "What are you doing here, Elijah?"

And he said, "I have been very zealous for the Lord God of hosts; because the children of Israel have forsaken Your covenant, torn down Your altars, and killed Your prophets with the sword. I alone am left, and they seek to take my life."

Then the Lord said to him: "Go, return on your way to the Wilderness of Damascus; and when you arrive, anoint Hazael as king over Syria. Also, you shall anoint Jehu the son of Nimshi as king over Israel. And Elisha the son of Shaphat of Abel Meholah you shall anoint as prophet in your place. It shall be that whoever escapes the sword of Hazael, Jehu will kill; and whoever escapes the sword of Jehu, Elisha will kill. Yet I have reserved seven thousand in Israel, all whose knees have not bowed to Baal, and every mouth that has not kissed him." So he departed from there.

1. God addressed Elijah's physical needs.

What took place next is clinical. God met Elijah right where he was and began to restore him in body, soul, and spirit. The Great Physician became Elijah's nutritionist, psychologist, and Lord.

First, God addressed Elijah physically. Elijah was standing before God, frightened and in despair, yet God said nothing. "Then he laid down under the tree, and he fell asleep" (1 Kings 19:5-9). God simply let his devoted and exhausted Prophet rest. With this, God allows us to see that when we're fatigued, we're more susceptible to satanic delusion. Satan wants to keep us all from getting the rest we require to maintain our health and sanity. We get so busy doing God's work at times, that we fail to take breaks for personal rest and worship. We're often pulled and pushed in too many directions. Not because we're any busier than the generation that came before us; usually it's because we have loaded our plate with things that God never intended for us to do.

The Scriptures say that bodily exercise profits a little (1 Timothy 4:8). I believe that our spiritual usefulness, which is important, is enhanced by our taking care of our physical bodies. After all, the body is the temple of the Lord and He deserves a palace rather than a run down shack.

We intuitively know we should take care of our bodies, but often fail to do it. After Elijah had slept, God fed him. Elijah slept some more and God fed him again. In I Kings 19:7-8, the angel of the Lord told Elijah, "Get up and eat, for the journey is too much for you." This is not the first instance in which God prepared Elijah physically for ministry—we see it in I Kings 17:2-6 also. God took care of Elijah physically. Mighty Men take care of themselves physically.

2. God addressed Elijah psychologically.

After God fed Elijah and granted him much needed rest, He sent Elijah to stand on a mountain, for He was about to pass by him. As he did this, a mighty wind began to blow. It was shaking and pulling trees up by the roots. But Elijah discovered that God was not in the wind. Then the earth began to shake. Rocks started falling, and the earth split open near his feet. But Elijah discovered that God was not in the earthquake. Then there came a fire. It engulfed everything around Elijah. But again, when he searched for God, He was not in the fire.

Finally, after those three dramatic acts of nature, Elijah heard a gentle whisper, and there Elijah discovered God. The Lord asked him one probing and convicting question: "What are you doing here, Elijah?" Make no mistake here, God, who knows everything, was not searching for information, but rather to make a point.

Elijah began rattling off all the great things he had done as if to impress the Lord of Hosts. How foolish…but everyone does and says foolish things when we are in the process of running from the Lord.

Elijah essentially said: "Lord, I stood against the prophets; I am the only one out there that cares; don't you know what I've done for you? I think I've done enough; I've done my time!"

Jesus said, "You shall know the truth, and the truth shall set you free" (John 8:32). Elijah is about to get a dose of reality from God.

3. God addressed Elijah's pride.

God never responded to the litany of Elijah's accomplishments. It's as if God is saying, "Of course you did those things; I empowered, protected and sent you!" Instead of a response to Elijah, God gave him his next assignment. "Go back out the way you came and anoint two kings and a prophet" (19:15).

Elijah obeyed, without comment. God did not rail about Elijah's disobedience, after all, does the Scripture not tell us that once we repent, our sins are separated from us as far as the East is from the West, to be remembered against us no more (Psalm 103:11-12)? God essentially told Elijah, "You've got work to do." God wasn't finished with Elijah; in fact, his most important work was yet to come.

God also reminded Elijah to humble himself. After all, He still had 7,000 other people who had as much courage and conviction as Elijah. He was telling Elijah in those verses, "I do not need you to accomplish my work, but I want you." That is so precious and real for each of us as well. God wants you to become a Mighty Man because He loves you!

People often tell me their desire for a friend or family member to come to know Christ. They intimate that they wish this person could get saved because he or she has so much to offer. However, I correct them as gently as I can, saying, "No, that individual has nothing to offer that God needs. Great gifts and abilities often keep people from coming to Jesus." None of us has anything that God needs.

God just wants us. We're important to God, not for what we bring to Him but rather because He genuinely loves us.

4. God gives Elijah some advice.

God told him to get a helper named Elisha and train him. It's never good for any man to be alone continuously. God recognized that he needed an encourager and co-laborer to stand with him and be mentored by him.

Obedience is essential in overcoming the three D's: A lesson for today.

Restored by God, Elijah went forward to anoint two kings, train a prophet and become a servant to those 7,000 faithful followers. Now, let's look at a contemporary and notable example of a successful businessman who faced defeat, discouragement, and despair, the devil's "3D's," and overcame them.

Tom Monaghan started Domino's Pizza with his brother in the early 1960s with just 900 borrowed dollars. They bought a small pizzeria and began delivering pizzas to a college dorm. It was an instant success, especially after they started using an innovative corrugated box that kept the pies hot. After trading a Volkswagen Beetle to his brother for his half of the business, Tom went on a tear, opening outlet after outlet. In 1985, he opened 900 Domino's Pizza stores.

At the time, there was nothing equivalent in the history of the American free enterprise system. No one—not even McDonald's—had ever opened 900 franchises in a year.

To say Mr. Monaghan was a financial success is an understatement. As rich as King Midas, he bought the Detroit Tigers in 1983. A year later, the Tigers won the World Series. He purchased a large lakeside resort, plus several airplanes and over 200 cars, including Duesenberg's, Rolls Royces and a 1929 Bugatti Royale that alone cost $8.1 million.

Mr. Monaghan started giving money to mission projects, in keeping with his Christian faith. He got so involved in projects in Honduras that he sensed a call to full-time ministry there and made preparations to pursue it full-time. But because he had neglected his business, when he put it on the market, no one would buy it, at least not for anything near what it was worth. Competitors were popping up everywhere, and he had lost the cutting edge that made him so successful. Many of his stores were no longer profitable, and everything around him was suddenly turning sour. The devil's "3 D's" showed up, attacking Mr. Monaghan.

In the midst of all of this gloom, he picked up the classic book by C.S. Lewis, *Mere Christianity*. By the eighth chapter, Monaghan was convicted that pride—the deadliest of all sins—had overtaken him. He stopped everything and began pursuing God again, in earnest. By now, his nights were sleepless, and he had lost his focus. There was no joy, no happiness. Then he broke through in prayer and repentance. "From this moment on I decided that I would focus on God, family and Domino's," he wrote.

Rearranging his priorities, he fired several layers of management and closed down unprofitable stores. He honed his knowledge of computers and networking and brought the company up to date. By 1993, gross receipts were $2.3 billion, and he was personally making more than $3 million per month. He had gone from success to disaster to incredible success again—because he recognized that pride goes before the fall, and he did something about it.

Like Elijah, he got things back in order, putting God in first place. Mr. Monaghan became a Mighty Man.

Now, that's a rather dramatic example, but the principles Monaghan had to learn are the same for all men, whether we make millions or less than $20,000 a year: it must be God, family, and our work, in that order. God has uniquely prepared and equipped each of us, but we must do our part by submitting all we are to Him. He demands and deserves first place in our hearts. Anything less is courting disaster.

Are you facing the "3 D's," defeat, discouragement, and despair? Healthy self-evaluation is good. Success in life follows re-enlistment after defeat. In Elijah's case, his greatest achievements in life followed his biggest failure. God is a God of the second chance.

When we face a crisis, we need to remember what God has done and will do for us. We need to remember to pursue Him with our whole heart. And, we need to remember those who need us. We must refrain from looking for the sandpit and trust God to help us finish the race well.

Instead of getting sidetracked by all the theatrics of life, we must listen for His gentle whisper to our hearts. We can hear it, but only when we're serious about getting into God's word, continuing in prayer, and staying in fellowship with other believers.

How do we handle defeat, discouragement, and despair? By looking unto Jesus, the author, and finisher of our faith. (Hebrews 12:2) Is God whispering that He wants you to become a Mighty Man? I think He is!

Appendix One

A PLACE OF NO PAIN

On Wednesday morning, October 27,
2004, our Kathryn went to Heaven.
Between 7 AM and 7:15,
She left us for Jesus and places unseen.
But she did not leave us without any hope;
For everywhere we look we discover more notes,
That she wrote down on paper while depression she fought.
She leaned on her Savior in word and in thought.
She learned how to worship while fighting to live.
She learned how to love, how to pray and to give.
Each day was a labor with less sunshine than rain;
But now she's with Jesus in the place of no pain.

At 25 some say her life was cut short.
That her prayers went unanswered and even ignored.
But to those who were privileged to know her up close,'
There is evidence abundant that she was the choice;
Of a God who responded to her greatest obsession.
To know Him and love Him with reckless abandon.
Hundreds of pages of journals of prayer,
Assure us that Kathryn is living up there.
Praising Her Savior with thousands of Saints,
Her victory secured in the place of no pain.

The sorrow of loss crashes into our lives;
When we least expect it, we suddenly cry.
But quickly our Lord gathers us unto Himself,
And reminds us that Kathryn, at last, has her health.
She's running the race that she cannot lose;
We move forward with life and despair we refuse.
We know where she is, and we know how to find her.
We live each day with this blessed reminder.
To live is Christ and to die is gain.
New life, forever, in a place of no pain.
RWS

THE EAGLE FLIES

Eighteen days after sweet Kathryn died,
The gentle Savior came alongside
Of Tommye and me as we traveled to cheer
A friend who lost a loved one so dear.

Struck down on a foreign field was he,
While serving his country to keep us free.
Like Kathryn, he died at 25,
Making the ultimate sacrifice.

On the fields of Iraq, he committed all,
For a cause he believed in, this soldier stood tall.
It's oft repeated that freedom's not free.
Byron Trotter died for you and me.

As we processed our grief consoling each other,
Missing our daughter as a Father and Mother.
We passed a vulture signaling death,
And without a word I took a breath.

My heart began to sink in despair,
But I heard a voice say, 'Son I care
More for you than you've ever understood.
My thoughts toward you are always good.'

'Child, have you forgotten that the day before
Kathryn died, she was longing for more.
She often spoke of how Eagles soar,
And prayed for the day when she'd suffer no more.'

'So I showed you and Tommye a curious site.
You stopped to admire it, so regal and bright.
A beautiful Eagle perched so high,
Displayed in majesty, his backdrop, the sky!

'You both enjoyed this scene for the time,
But neither of you knew what I had in mind.
I was granting you the assurance you'd need,
When today by faith you planted a seed.

'Of hope and compassion for others who cried;
Sharing your experience while trying to deny,
How painfully deep you were hurting inside,
With all those questions that begin with 'Why.'

'I am the God of Infinite detail;
I am the God who can not fail;
I am He who understands;
I am He with Sovereign plans.

'If you are willing to place your faith,
Unreservedly in my Wisdom and Grace,
I'll allow your faith to become your sight.
My peace will displace your darkest night.

'When you saw the eagle that day,
Before Kathryn Anne was called away;
I was carefully showing you,
That Kathryn's dream would soon come true.

'They that wait upon the Lord,
Will always be renewed, restored.
On Eagle's wings, Kathryn came to me;
No longer weary, finally free.

'So take my rest, my burden's light.
I bear it with you in the night.
While Kathryn left you for a while,
Today she wears a forever smile.

'When you see an eagle soar,
Think of Kathryn and cherish more,
The life she lives with no more pain,
To live is Christ, and to die is gain.'

—rws

DR. RICK SCARBOROUGH

From 1990 to June 2002, Dr. Scarborough was the Senior Pastor of First Baptist Church of Pearland located on the southeast side of the Houston Metroplex. In 1992, he gained national recognition when he exposed the contents of a disturbing assembly program at the local high school. Under the auspices of an "AIDS Presentation," a young lady, sponsored by the AIDS Foundation of Houston, candidly discussed every sex act imaginable expressing the opinion (presented as fact) that "safe sex" was attainable by using condoms. Dr. Scarborough recorded the assembly and then made transcripts available to his congregation the following Sunday morning. The resulting furor that erupted caught the eye of the national media.

Dr. Scarborough mobilized his congregation during the following months to make significant changes in Pearland. Members began running for public office, as well as volunteering for various organizations beyond traditional "Christian ministry" seeking to become "salt and light" in their community.

In 1998, he founded Vision America, an organization whose mission is to "inform and mobilize Pastors and their congregations to become salt and light, becoming pro-active in restoring Judeo-Christian values in America."

Dr. Scarborough's work has been featured in numerous articles and publications around the nation. A partial listing includes the *New York Times, Washington Times, Kansas City Star, Dallas Morning News, Houston Chronicle, Boston Globe* and the *Congressional Quarterly*.

Dr. Scarborough has appeared on *Larry King Live*, Fox News, CBS Evening News and numerous other television and radio programs. The work of Vision America has been featured in several documentaries and specials such as CNN's award winning special, *God's Warriors* and the HBO documentary, *Friends of God*.

Dr. Scarborough is author of the widely acclaimed and appropriately entitled book, *Enough is Enough; a Call to Christian Involvement*. In 2008 he published an updated edition of *Enough is Enough*. Other published works include, *Mixing Church and State God's Way* and *It All Depends on What Is...Is*. He also published *Liberalism Kills Kids* and contributed two chapters to *Judicial Tyranny*, along with such noted authors as James Dobson, former US Attorney General Edwin Meece, and Alabama Supreme Court Chief Justice Roy Moore. Dr. Scarborough regularly speaks in churches, rallies, and political conventions.

Scheduling information and availability for Dr. Scarborough to speak, or conduct a Mighty Men Weekend or Mighty Men Day, can be obtained by calling:

(866)522-5582
Monday through Friday, from
8:30AM until 5:00 PM Central.

NOTES